HEAVEN'S BETTER

A JOLLY LOOK AT MIRACLES AND ENTREPRENEURSHIP

HENRY A. WALTER

ISBN: 1477498230

ISBN-13: 9781477498231

Chapter 1

It was February 25, 1937 in Oklahoma, a most inauspicious day. The Dust Bowl was still a fact of life although there were signs of relief beginning to peek through the gravy-brown air.

The Great Depression was still grinding people down with hope still hidden by blowing dust. Few folks were worrying about obesity; skin and bones seemed to take precedence in the workaday world.

Countries around the world were gathering to hold another war, World War II that would involve most of the planet. Had I had a choice, I might have decided to wait a few years, hoping for a brighter outlook in this old world. That day, right smack in the middle of the dustbowl, I wandered innocently into the world.

Born of parents John and Willa Walter, I entered the tussle of searching for a decent life. I had lots of competition. Most of the world's population was struggling for food, always on the brink of failure, generally living on two ounces of rice per day, if they could find it.

Things didn't look hopeful. Eight out of ten men had a job but few that paid well. The others could only pray the government would find a way back to prosperity or scope out the whole country for a place to raise a family, maybe loping along the rail tracks trying to get a ride to heaven or hell; neither destination seemingly within easy reach.

It seemed as if only a miracle could get America and the rest of the troubled world out of the mess we had made of our world.

A man or woman could only console themselves that someday things had to get better but the waiting seemed endless. The dust clouds just kept coming over arid farm fields that hadn't seen raindrops for several years.

But the miracles stayed hidden behind the smothering dirt. Were we just too miserable to depend upon "supernatural assistance?" Is there the possibility that we could have helped ourselves a bit by recognizing and acknowledging that miracles really do happen and, if we would have accepted God's help, might our attitudes have been raised to levels far above the woes we faced daily?

I am sure of it. And as I matured, I saw evidence of divine aid. It was hard to understand, even though I believed in God, He could and would offer a door into the dustless sunlight of daily life. But I finally got it; sure enough, it had been there all the time.

Just about four years ago, I experienced a miracle. It was a vivid moment, clear as a bell. It wasn't the first time for me. But this particular miracle, unlike others throughout my life, registered immediately; something had occurred that was different.

My wife and I were walking to the school parking lot after attending my six-year-old grandson's first grade musical program. The boy had had a part in the performance so I was feeling pretty good. In fact, everything was good; business, health, even the stock market was up. Life was good.

As we were approaching the lot, a young boy, about twelve or so, passed close by me. He had a basketball under his arm. Although our eyes didn't meet, as he passed, I heard a voice. Yep, I really heard a voice say "Heaven's better."

It wasn't a "royal" announcement. Just an unequivocally precise thought.

I don't recall ever hearing an inner voice so clearly. Well, sure, I've had thoughts and memories of conversations and maybe even my conscience has broken through a few times. (My conscience doesn't say anything; it just groans.) But this was nothing like I had ever encountered before and I realized something extraordinary had occurred.

Carolyn and I walked to our car but the sparkle stayed with me. Where had those two words come from? Why did that precise thought waltz through my mind at that moment? I tried to remember what I might have been thinking. Nothing. My mind had been "at ease" as far as I could recollect. I hardly noticed that boy; just someone passing by.

That night I mulled the phrase over and for several days thereafter. Why had it been so vivid? What could have prompted such an odd brainwave at that specific instant when the only thing I probably was thinking how cold it was that February evening.

About a week later, as quick as a swallow of cold water, it came to me. The little boy reminded me of myself at that age. I don't know why, but I saw myself in that boy who looked nothing like the photos of me at that marvelous age.

From that day forward my life was changed. First in little bites, then bigger and bigger. I was able to finally turn control of my life over to God. The biggest obstacle in my life, and I suspect in the lives of most who are looking for a way to handle life in this turbulent world, had been the inability to let go; to trust, to believe (or at least have a strong supposition) that God is dependable enough to trust. That He really will watch out for my welfare and those I love—if I let Him.

Even more, somewhere in my subconscious, I knew for the first time and most assuredly that God would do a much better job managing a doubting me than I'd done over the past 70-plus years. As the days moved forward, I began to sense changes in my attitude and perceive a widened life around me. Sure and I was frightened, a bit uneasy because my heart and mind couldn't absorb the enormity of what might be happening to me.

During those same several days, it occurred to me that my twelfth year had always harbored the best of the best of my memories. Turning twelve was a time before the walloping confusion of puberty, a time of all fun and no responsibilities. It was the year of my only birthday party, the year I got my Red Ryder BB gun. I also received a knit shirt from my best friend. I loved it so; I wore it until I caught it on a wayfaring nail and unraveled the whole right sleeve.

It was a year of joyous encounters, as I recall, with nothing to fear but the ghost stories kids will tell each other.

I grew up in the little town of Loveland, Colorado from about 1940 through 1955. Estimates were that almost five thousand lucky citizens made the town "...a little "Camelot, but we didn't know it," as voiced by one of my classmates at our fortieth high school reunion.

All I recall about those earlier years was having fun with my friends and eating mom's wonderful fried taters and beans. I was too young to be affected by the news of the coming World War II. Or that we were still in the Great Depression and like everyone else we were poor.

Life was not at all a series of gloomy days and monotony. In fact, growing up in that small town of Loveland, Colorado, was maybe the best world any youngster could inhabit to spread his wings and enjoy the life God gave him or her. We had an innate compulsion toward exploration without fear of consequences. In those halcyon days, school teachers saw no need to caution us against what consequences might drop on us. Mom and dad didn't preach much. In fact, the only news about God we got in Sunday School at the old First Baptist Church. It wasn't that we were non-believers; we just accepted that God was there and we just sort of let things be. And "miracle" was a word I had no relationship with until years later.

The Great Depression was still grinding folks down in 1937, and the dust bowl was still layering people's lives with its grimy fog of desperation. President Roosevelt was airing his fireside chats on the radio, telling us things were getting better—but they weren't much. Americans were looking for miracles but maybe those dust clouds and empty stomachs took so much of our time it was hard to look for blessings and ignore the world's daily vexations.

Soon there was World War II to suffer through as Germany's Hitler and Japan's Tojo threatened to take over the world. The miracle of American resilience saved the world—barely. Folks were more than ready to work hard. Work had been sort of scarce for almost a decade. We had the energy, the grit and the desire, along with patriotism to stir our souls.

Each day was new and inviting. I was like a little kitten: Each morning I awakened to a new and untroubled world. It was fun to get up, hurry through breakfast and get outside to see what my older brothers and sisters had lined up for the day. As I grew (figuratively speaking; I never attained more than five-feet-five-point-five stature) I accepted life as it was handed to me. Never once did I say thank you for the blessings I received day after day.

But God understood my unawareness and in later years, He reminded me and my senior years have been just as happy as that twelve-year-old experienced. Thankfulness can be healing.

My twelfth year had such an impact on my later life, I later wrote a newspaper column about growing up in a small town in the Fifties. I had watched a talking head on TV one evening and his hypothesis was that the Fifties must have been boring. My ears pricked up; what was he thinking? Maybe he was a child of the sixties, you know, when teens and young "adults" seemed to need outside stimulation. I had to set the record straight. So I wrote a newspaper column to set him straight.

> *Didn't know, didn't care*
> *I recollect one morning when the radio announced the beginning of the Korean Conflict (those fighting it considered it a "war"). Boring? Could have fooled us kids. I know I said a prayer because my older brothers were of draft age. I even*

promised God that He could "have" me when I turned sixty if He would stop the war.

In 1950, my gang didn't have time to be bored. We played unsupervised baseball, swam in the untreated water of the irrigation ditch, hiked into the foothills and camped (no adults allowed), enjoyed long bike rides, sans helmets, in the country so lovingly surrounding our little community. We had gobs of places to play and we found 'em all.

And we had paper fights! Ten or fifteen of us were paper boys delivering the local newspaper and especially in the summer, since there were no organized activities to speak of, we clobbered each other for hours. Oh, those fights were beauts and as far as I can remember, no one got killed. On summer days, we'd gather early before the latest edition was off the press. There was this great big stack of previous editions in the press room and we could "borrow" as many as we needed. Recycling as yet was unneeded. We used things up a whole lot better than today.

We had the greatest arena for which a budding gladiator could ever hope for. Loveland had a pickle factory with big wooden vats about twelve feet across and eight feet high. A wooden walkway wound around the top of the vats where the pickle workers stirred the brine soaking the pickles. It formed a perfect roof under which sneaking was a twilight adventure for a six-to-ten-year-old with warrior visions because beneath the walkways there were these wondrous tunnels between the vats.

We'd fold the old papers into a five by five square that could be flung about twenty-five yards with some accuracy. Then we'd load up and hie ourselves to the pickle barrels, choose up sides and have the momma of all wars. If you got hit, you were out of the game. There wasn't much arguing because those tightly folded little squares were as hard as a board and would make a Thwack! that could be heard by everybody.

Later (this was before daylight savings time) we'd go swimming or maybe take in a movie at the Rialto Theater (we collected used pop bottles and sold them to Ted's Grocery at two cents apiece and 14 cents would get you a ticket allowing you to stay until the projectionist shut things down.)

Now, just so you won't think we were brawl-ers with no self-esteem (didn't know, didn't care), we were resourceful. Most times when one of us was "wounded," we'd sneak some band-aids from somebody's house and cover the bleeding so moms wouldn't get upset. If you got whacked where it showed, you lied, and mom didn't sweat it as long as we were able to scoot ourselves up to the supper table.

I can't think of a time boredom entered into our childhood equations. There was just too much to do. Like this was farm country and most farmers had cows, some with bulls. There were Billy goats who were just naturally offended when we got too close. And they liked to chase cocky dumb kids who believed a fence was for climbing over. Yeah, we did and only got caught once by the farmer. That was when we learned he was crankier than the bulls or goats.

We were free to imitate cowboys or Indians or whatever new war or turmoil was featured on the movie newsreels. We only retreated when the Billy goat or bull got too close.

We always chummed with at least one lucky guy who had a pup tent—most of us couldn't afford one. We'd ride our bikes up to the foot of the foothills and climb our own "Mt. Everest" (it was called Marianna's Butte—just high enough that you could see the "bad guys" coming).

We'd cook up some pork'n beans and hotdogs and sit around the campfire telling stories about what we were gonna do if we grew up. As was and inevitable behavior of twelve-year-old boys, those beans got the best of us. Before long, the first bean gas made its way back into the world and "The Sound of Music" wafted through the valley.

Mother Nature's wind was more accommodating in those days. It never blew any roofs away that I recall, but it provided the "fuel" for some of our longest bike rides. We'd rig a stick inside our jacket shoulders to make a sort of sail, put our feet up on the handlebars and cruise for a mile or more. It was hard work riding against the wind to get home and sometimes we missed supper. It was worth the whack on the butt. I still love a windy night.

We didn't hear our parents complain much about boredom either. 'Course there weren't any 40-hour weeks so if they got bored, it must've been while they worked. Now that I think back on it, I'm not so sure our folks didn't like working fifty or sixty hours a week. They sure seemed to spend 'nawful lot of time at it.

Okay, maybe it was dull times, but we enjoyed lots of leisure because our parents didn't sign us up for tennis lessons or dance class.

-30-

All this marvelous and delightful reminiscing brought me back to the question: Is heaven better than the best year of my life?

Why would I receive such a message? I was and am just an ordinary guy with no discernable gift of eerie mental capacity. In fact, for much of my younger life I wasn't especially aware of anything going on around me. But there it was, an intuitive message too clear to ignore.

I spent a day or two trying to shrug off the words because things like that are for those who are very religious. I had been just a casual spectator at The First Baptist Church.

It was a fleeting moment but because it seemed so momentous; my id, ego and superego felt all tangled up. Was it words from the devil and I was being misled into thinking I was someone extraordinary?

It couldn't be. If the devil was playing games, he certainly wouldn't be touting God's own heaven. I mean, you don't give your opponent good publicity.

I was seventy when that voice cried out in the wilderness of my mind. I'm seventy-five now and since then I haven't heard any more "peculiar" messages. I admit that with a certain relief for now I can presume, with some certainty, it was not senility whispering absurd nothings in my ear that cold evening.

The "thought" wouldn't go away, though. It got to where I was worried my friends and coworkers were counting how many times I argued with myself as that moment became more and more firmly imbedded in a feeling of belief. It came and it went. Of course, I used a lot of energy trying to rebut the motive of this strange gift.

As I mentally debated I slowly began to accept this bubble in my mind (and heart) that wouldn't burst.

Chapter 2

I don't recall the first miracle by which I was blessed. I was busy being born and probably had mother's milk on my mind. Nevertheless, I believe my birth a miracle; it wasn't because I was good at geography. I was born and raised in America and I've artlessly accepted my right to food, good health and a cool clear glass of water as though they were as ordinary as a politician's promise.

What are the odds of such a fortuitous birth? As of October 2011, the world population estimate was about seven billion. The U.S. population was near 330 million. Using my math, that means each one of us had a ninety-six percent chance that we would be struggling every day of our lives just to survive in a Third World country! The overwhelming majority of people in our world are too busy trying to find something to eat while hiding from the secret police.

I've never experienced a really hungry day. So, in contrast to the misfortune of our foreign brothers and sisters, why then don't we, the "lucky" few, dearly appreciate our unique blessings?

I think we Americans regularly accept that "miracles" in and of our lives are nothing more than lucky breaks or coincidences? That conclusion begs the question that luck runs both ways and coincidences depend upon chance? It is no wonder we can't find the answer for all of our worrying about the future.

Luck and coincidences come with no guarantees. They are a one-day wonder. Miracles come with a platinum bound guarantee—if we can learn to acknowledge them. A miracle is a blessing, yes, but the greater reward may come after the fact: The possibility that there is some place where that miracle may have been "mailed" to us.

In my case, it took years for the seed of wonderment to take root and grow. I have lived the good life but there was, as St. Paul said, still a thorn in my side. I could not accept the notion that giving my life to God was the smart thing to do. What if God wanted me to be something I didn't want to be? That's a big risk most of us are unwilling to take. It can be downright scary, giving up self control.

In fact, it's impossible to surrender your life's trust to another if you don't have some background to gain reassurance in that Person—God. How'm I gonna do that? is the real challenge.

Even if life seems miserable it's still your life, an asset not easily given away. Shoot, there's always a chance we'll win the lottery and the world will be ours. And if life is good, who in his or her right mind is going to trade it for some unknown—and perhaps a non-existent future?

The only thing that will change our mind is faith. Reliance on something or someone bigger than us, more powerful than all the guarantees the politicians can dream up.

It's just too big a gamble, we tell ourselves, letting go of what we've got hold of before we have something else to grab onto is not what the wise, logic-driven folks are going to do. We can't do it! Not without some assurance the contract is valid. Where's the insurance covering this big venture of letting go of our lives to take a walk on an unknown, new trail?

I think this is one of those instances where God's gift of free will has become a struggle. We willingly take the path of frailty and fallibility when we can't let ourselves enjoy the fruits of this life. What a wonderful life this would be if we had courage to overcome adversity; if we had the ability to not worry over things we can't control; struggling with decisions we must make using only our own ego driven intellect.

If I've learned anything, it has been if I can't let go in the struggle to gain tranquility in my life, I'm doomed to despair.

If I can let go, I stand to gain everything that is good in life. I will be brave where before I was timid. I gain optimism where I was uncertain before. I will find confidence in my relationship others. And maybe most importantly, if I let God do my worrying for me, I'll never again be reluctant to forge ahead with my plans, my goals, my dreams.

Thank God, I was able to let go before my whole life was used up and I had some time to enjoy... Since that undeniable and almost perfect transformation I have experienced even more "bonuses" in my life. I no longer suffer from a life-long inferiority complex. Today, I have a sense of self-confidence, I can take on more exigent tasks, such as becoming the president of my church congregation—meaning I can to stand before one hundred people and give a talk/speech/explanation or maybe even an apology for messing up a task.

I'm also no longer hesitant to ask questions or speak my mind in a large group meeting. Heck, I don't even worry whether my fly is open.

But I can do all those things now although I couldn't for the first sixty years of my life. Hard to believe? Yes, indeed, I shiver at times with the realization what God has enabled me to achieve.

Chapter 3

One thing just led to another as I began to accept the impossibility of explaining why good things happened the way they did. But they did happen and now I'm glad although sometimes I never felt a change until months, sometimes years later. Now that I think about it, I am able to reconstruct some happenings that led to other "happenings" that worked out better than I'd ever dreamed. Why did I end up at this or that job that may have led to another particular job that was more to my liking? Coincidence just doesn't offer enough "meat" to explain it all.

Miracles can happen almost every day. Do you remember the last time; that little piece of good luck that you shrugged off?

But if you had thought about it, explored the moment, you might have come very close to an inkling God is with you. That Jesus really does care and the Holy Spirit does indeed take a hand in your life. The old song, "Little Things (can) Mean a Lot" was written for teenage lovers but a whole lifetime can profit from its promise.

As I look back on all those "little" miracles I missed, one really serious flirt with death comes back. There was that winter when I was about twelve. Dad and one of his friends took me on my first deer hunting trip. Coming back, there was an unexpected curve followed by a long, icy hill. On the right side of the road, the mountain dropped off what to me looked like a sure way to avoid puberty.

Dad wasn't going fast but the combination of hillcrest and winding downhill on a snow-covered road worked against him. The car spun out, the right rear—just where I was cringing while staring at that drop-off to eternal rigidity. Dad never touched the brakes. He let the car slide and stroked the steering wheel slightly to the left and we rolled slowly right across that road and into the culvert on the life-enhancing uphill side.

We got the car pushed back onto the road and drove into Fort Collins where we stopped at a restaurant for a cuppa. I got out of the car and suddenly my knees were bonking against each other. I tried to take a deep breath and found there was none of that famous Rocky Mountain air available. I was shaking like a mountain quaky and I couldn't seem to get a grip on the door handle to let myself faint in a twelve-year-old masculine manner worthy of Tom Sawyer.

I just sorta whoozed back and forth as I grasped what could have happened an hour ago. Dad came around the car and pulled me up by the arm, kinda carrying me along like a sack of pooped night crawlers. As we were sitting at the counter and I was rattling my cup and saucer all frazzely, dad put his arm around my shoulder and said, "It wasn't even close, Hank. I knew the car would slide the other way." That was the moment when I knew dad was watertight. Nothing could sink him and nothing ever did.

I'm sure many people experience one of my most consistent curses; the feeling of wanting to be somewhere else, doing something different. That feeling has followed me into adulthood. Pleasure was just out of reach.

Dissatisfaction is a most unrewarding state of mind. It makes you think negatively, a deep down fear that nothing is really fun or fulfilling. It fashions your life, whether you know it or not, and the sense of having fun becomes more and more remote.

That little boy and his basketball brought back all those memories. Now, Something—Someone— had told me that heaven is better? I just wish I hadn't wasted so much time timorously wondering if I had really heard it. There is no way in this world those two words, "Heaven's better," could have been anything but a miracle. It was a promise that is bringing comfort to the rest of my life.

The reality of miracles is disconcerting to Americans. There's a mysticism there that makes us uncomfortable in the secular, logical world of our settled experience. In fact, I'm sure even longtime Christians still have a problem with the miracle of Christ's birth.

Chapter 4

We were poor but so was everyone else, so we didn't have much gripe about what we did not have. What we did have, most of us anyway, was three square meals a day, warm clothes, a home with enough beds for everyone and a real sense of pride in America, the land of the free and the home of the brave. The only drug that was a problem is we didn't yet have Doctor Jonas Salk's polio vaccine and some of my friends came down that dastardly disease.

Growing up poor became an advantage later in life. Maybe it was only a little miracle, but since our folks didn't have much left over after filling the pot with potatoes and whatever grew in the Victory

Gardens, we had to improvise. Luxuries were only something seen in movie theaters…like the fancy cars driven by movie stars. That life was so strange most folks accepted the great divide from the rich and famous.

Part of that was making our own toys. One of my older brothers was a craftsman, making World War II model weapons out of scrap wood and Campbell's soup cans. He made toy guns that our soldiers were using in a more serious way. One machine gun, I recall, would have passed for a "spittin' image" of those used by the GIs to save democracy. If I ever touched one of his creations without permission, though, it was a race across our long front lawn, him throwing rocks and me ducking. (I could pretty much outrun everyone in the neighborhood, but it took my brother several years to give up.)

After WW II, there was this time that a lot of war surplus was available for not much more than a mouthful of bubblegum. In 1946, the local drugstore got in a shipment of war surplus military gas masks. We were all out doing our thing one day when one of the neighbor boys came running over to tell us that W&T had these gas masks for about a dollar apiece. For the little kids' size, it was seventy-five cents, I think.

We were ready for anything new and exciting—if it was cheap. There was a run on W&T Pharmacy for about two days until every one of those masks was gone. Kids were mowing lawns without being scourged to instill the work ethic. We were trading anything that might make a nickel at the junk yard. There wasn't an unclaimed empty pop bottle in the whole town.

My dad, John quit school after the eighth grade to learn to be an auto body repairman. He'd had enough of picking cotton, I guess, so he took an apprenticeship in Oklahoma City at fifty cents a day to learn the trade. He once told me he slept above the repair shop where he interned and, for a nickel, could go across the street to a restaurant each night after closing hours and get the leftovers. I don't know how many years he did that, but he ended up as one of the premier tin peckers in that part of the country.

Mom (Willa Alma) was working as a telephone operator when she and dad got married in 1927. Story she told was she and another young lady had set their bonnets for "Gentleman John" Walter. So what they did was they had a footrace to see who would pursue the gent. Willa won, which may be why I turned out to be a swift runner until my legs got too short to keep up the taller kids. I can't be sure that race resulted in a miracle but I was sure blessed with a great mom and dad.

I was the sixth of eight siblings (later when two other brothers unexpectedly showed up, dad used to brag he had two and a half dozen kids—two girls and six boys), but I may have been a surprise. Although my mom swore I was born on February 25, my birth certificate said February 27. It may have been all that dust swirling around Oklahoma and they didn't realize I was there for two whole days, but it sure caused a whale of a problem sixty-five years later when I tried to register for Social Security benefits. I didn't retire for five years because it took that long for the government to admit I really had been paying that FICA all those years. I guess they just couldn't find the money.

Soon after they were married, the Depression and the dust bowl came along which didn't allow much leeway in career building in those days. Mostly people were just looking for some fresh air. But dad persevered, learned his trade and opened his own body shop in Edmond, Oklahoma, where I was born. He worked at it for some years, building his own house—and making a lot of friends because he was repairing their jalopies knowing they wouldn't be able to pay for until it rained, which it didn't.

Anyway, the economics of the situation finally couldn't be tolerated any longer (every working man was dirt poor—no kidding). In 1939 dad finally locked up the automobile repair business, packed up the family and moved to Cheyenne, Wyoming, where we lived a couple years. It wasn't "Grapes of Wrath," but it sure wasn't happy wandering. I can only imagine how disappointed and discouraging it must have been for my folks but there just didn't seem to be any miracles available right then.

Then Dad got an offer from Knox Chevrolet in Loveland, Colorado, about 60 miles down the road from Cheyenne, to manage the body shop there and we moved. It was soon after Pearl Harbor and, as could be expected, things picked up business wise. Dad soon became known as the best repairman in Northern Colorado and the offers started coming in. He was the object of some energetic bidding around town and he soon went to work for the Studebaker dealership, then Kaiser-Frasier, then Hudson, all in Loveland.

Even though there was a war on and some were making money faster than the IRS could grab it, most families were still on the lean end of the wealth ratings and the few families that were wealthy knew enough not to brag or we might not patronize their bank or lumber yard if we ever did get some spending money.

Despite the black clouds presaging a world war, those were innocent times. In small towns nobody locked their car or house. I remember a sign along Highway 34 that hopefully said "5,000 by 1950." Today, I hear, it's about 65,000 or more. Bet they wish they had it to do over again. It's still a nice town, but not so small, that place where most folks didn't talk much about the family skeletons. They kept them close and maybe even treasured some if a rich uncle was involved.

The burglars knew we were slim pickin's and looked for better prospecting in Denver, another 50 miles down the road. And kids didn't have to be watched over so close which meant we didn't have supervised sports, at least not to the smothering extent of today. There were exceptions, of course. Once, while playing hard in the morning, I sprained my ankle. Thing was, I was one of the best "players" in town and I didn't want to miss a minute with my buddies. I favored the ankle until about mid afternoon. Then the opposite leg cramped up because I'd put too much strain on it. The guys helped me home and left me to explain to mom. I must have moaned extra large because it wasn't too long before she took me to the doctor, even if I wasn't bleeding. We were taken to the doctor only if mom couldn't get the bleeding stopped.

I had to cut the weeds in the cherry orchard for a whole month to pay for that doctor call. Doctors then weren't rich either—but they did get paid.

Chapter 5

My friends and I were unknowingly mentored by "The Greatest Generation," as Tom Brokaw so rightly dubbed them in his book. Our dads and moms were selected by God to live in an era of war and sorrow but they didn't waiver. Despite the struggles around the world, they continued to raise us as citizens pursuing an honorable demeanor. That they didn't give up was an undistinguished miracle to most.

Loveland was generally a town with plain, hard working souls that Brokaw highlights in his book. Folks with an itch to get it done (a failing art nowadays, what with old and new seminars taking up valuable space in our explorative minds.)

There was no TV to sophisticate us with uppity ideas about those in other places where people were "better off." One recollection that gives me a feeling of lost serenity was of Saturday afternoons and nights when neighbors parked along downtown's Fourth Street, the Main Gut, to do their shopping. Towards evening, our parents would give us a dime for a movie while they sat in their cars watching others stroll along the sidewalks window-shopping. It was also a good way to catch up on the gossip as many sat in friends and neighbor's cars to chat. (Front porches were okay for neighborhood catching-up, but you couldn't drive them downtown to share the really good chin-wagging with coverage from town limits to town limits.)

Folks were mostly ordinary, living a good if somewhat limited life. There was no crushing feeling that things were out of control except for the war and that was beginning to turn the Allies' way in 1943 and '44. It was a town that knew rock-steady life, such as east was "back East," west was "out West," north was "up North" and south was "down South." As long as one didn't get mixed up with trying to sort out why people spoke with an odd accent in all those directions, things sort of melded into an anticipated end-of-the-day tranquility.

One activity in the early 50s was standing in front of the Knox (same fella who sold Chevys) Furniture Store and stare at the black and white still photographs taped onto the front of that new-fangled thing called a television set. Live TV didn't hit the town until a few years later, but many Lovelanders were already experts. They'd studied that unmoving picture for months before the town doctor got the first set. Doc Vick, who I recall had the first TV set delivered to his home from Bob Hipps Appliances, invited a few of the "special" town folk to view his boob tube. The rest had to wait until an uncle or aunt had saved enough from Green Stamps to get their own set. But that was all later in the 50s after my generation had disappeared into the dour workday of the adult world. I've often wondered if TV diminished our work ethic; loafers now had something to occupy their mind, crowding out guilt.

We didn't have much in the way of luxuries. 'Nfact, we had what was known in those days as "didley squat." But we didn't go hungry and we had warm clothes. And maybe it was another miracle that our tummies weren't distended from malnutrition and bombs weren't being dropped on the local Woolworth Five and Dime. We didn't know how bad it could get for millions of kids having to grow up with whistling bombs and combating starvation during World War II—if they made it that far.

Our dads were working their buns off to make up for all the guys off fighting the war and moms were busy doing things the old fashioned way as they scrubbed clothes and tended Victory Gardens and saved big balls of tin foil for the war effort. And baked bread and canned fruit and mended clothes...

I went to Garfield "Garbage Can" Elementary through the second grade and then, after we moved into town—from the edge of town—I was transferred to Lincoln "Stinkin." I was scared to death. Those guys from Lincoln were tough. Not as tough as Washington "Washtub," but still I figured some guys were gonna show a new third grader how life worked. They were gonna beat the poop outta me just for fun. Since my momma was too busy canning tomatoes to accompany me to the new school it was up to pusillanimous me to alone confront those ruffians from the big school.

Sure enough, as I approached the front door, there was this kid sitting at the top of the steps.

I figured he was taking a smoke break or sharpening his switch blade, but there was no choice, no alternate route, no avoiding confrontation. I had to pass through that door. He stood as I timidly climbed those stairs. When I got to the top, now only a few feet away from a probable maiming, he said, "You're late!" I said I was not! I was a new student. "Hmph," he said, "That won't do you no good around here."

Just as I'd expected, my future would be filled with cowering, whimpering and lots of running. No one talked about self-esteem in those days. If you had it, no big deal, I guess. If you didn't, you walked home with a bunch of girls that would tell on the bullies.

Your third alternative was to become a hero and third grade provided few opportunities winning battle field medals.

I needed a miracle.

We had this thing called the city-wide track meet. We practiced from late April to late May, when the meet was held at the high school track. It was a big deal, running on the high school track where the big guys practiced. All three schools and junior high got the afternoon off to root their favorite athletes to victory.

I didn't distinguish this miracle until I was in late middle age. There was this guy, Irving, a big guy, a tough guy and a bully when he felt the urge. He could look at me and I'd wilt if there wasn't a shadow to hide in. It wasn't that Irving was fat; he just seemed to overflow on himself.

He was about, I think, six feet tall and weighed about 150 pounds. He was huge, he was imposing, and he was the worst nightmare of a seventy-five pound third grader. He was also the favorite in any athletic endeavor because no one challenged him. If you did, he'd sit on your head.

I was about knee high to a tall frog when I beat him in the 50-yards. I guess my teacher had noticed me running swiftly from shadow to shadow so Irving wouldn't pounce on me. But she urged me to enter the trials for the 50-yard-dash, Irving's race, so I did because I had a crush on her or something.

I beat everyone. I don't know what I expected from Irving. What he did was throw one huge arm around both my shoulders and say, "Hey, runt, you can run. You are swift! Let's go get a coke"

He became my unofficial bodyguard from that day forward until he left our school a couple years later. Irving was a mixed blessing. I don't think

I ever was at ease around him, even when he was telling everyone that "Hanky" was his little buddy and they better not mess with me. I've often wondered if Irving made it as a dentist. Despite his restraint on my behalf, he slipped now and then— he loved rearranging other peoples' teeth.

I did go on to win the third grade race that year against all comers in our town. Next year in the fourth grade I became aware of a new popularity. My self-esteem, although I didn't know it, also underwent such a boost that I was no longer afraid of any one in my class—unless they were girls.

That race stood out as an integral part of my "growing up." I was a winner and it felt marvelous. And fifty years down the road I think was another of those dinky things that made me believe in myself.

When we hit sixth grade, I still was unaware of my staturely impediment until a friend's mom pointed it out to me. Up to then I seemed able to play on an even par with my best friend, Eddie. Eddie and I played all sports, but now I felt the handicap. We played a lot of "h-o-r-s-e" basketball, you know, when guys went one on one to shoot baskets from different places on the court. The first guy took a shot and if he made it, the other had to shoot from the same spot. If the he missed, the first guy won an "h" and we then kept shooting until one had got all the letters of h-o-r-s-e, who was then winner.

My life became an absolute "H."

Chapter 6

We had these swell radio shows like "Terry and The Pirates" or "Jack Armstrong, the All American Boy." I don't recall any radio shows for girls; it was "Wheaties for Men!" Probably advertisers figured girls were busy learning to mend socks or reading dumb ol' books. I mean, y'know, girls were supposed to get married and do what their husbands told them to do so they wouldn't need the strong bodies like the real men us boys were going to grow into. Something like that, anyway.

TV for us came later but I think the radio shows left us to better use our imaginations. The stimulating plots a six- to twelve-year-old boy could conjure up listening to those shows were sure more interesting and exciting than the TV plots of today. We didn't just listen to our heroes; we were "living" their exploits. It was us wiping out the bad guys.

In sports, there was no such thing as "everyone plays whether they want to or not!" If you weren't good enough at some game, you looked for another at which you were good. I was terrible, but the guys allowed me to play baseball with them. Probably because I was fast and they figured I could run out most hits. (Problem was, I only got one hit in whole my Pee Wee career. I spent so much time on the bench, I learned to love wood, I guess, which is probably why my hobby in later years was woodworking.)

Loveland had two baseball fields and one coach/teacher/umpire and arbitrator. A local high school jock and future college president was great and we loved him. He taught us (well, most of us) fielding, hitting, running bases—everything we needed to know to pretend we were playing for the Denver Bears, at that time a farm team for the Yankees. That was where we learned to spit with accuracy.

I was unteachable. I was "bad field, no hit" my whole Pee Wee career—*except once*. Our team, Phinneys for Men, won the city championship one year and I actually helped out. See, I don't think in the three or four years I played I ever got a hit. I couldn't even bunt without getting smacked in the belly or the nose. It was okay, though. We accepted we couldn't all be winners and it didn't seem to stunt our self-esteem all that much. Being part of the bunch was important.

Anyway, the night of the big championship game, I was pitching, which meant they had to let me bat. Eddie was our catcher and he was the home run king of the league (about six teams). We also had a shortstop name of Ray (Red) Mehaffey who the coach rated as an "up and coming" Pee Wee Reese of the NY Yankees. Eddie went pro as an NFL defensive back. I think Ray fell in love with the forest and opted to spend his life as a Forest Ranger. The other guys who made life so much fun, baseball and otherwise, I can't recall as well.

Late in the game and the score was close. The other pitcher, "Hot Rod" Lampe walked Eddie, for an obvious reason; I, an automatic out all year, was next up.

Yeah, I punched one to right field. Eddie got to third and later scored. Don't remember if it was the winning run, but I've claimed it for nearly 60 years, by golly. My moment of fame didn't last long.

My folks did attend this game and were parked down the right field line. After the celebration, I raced my bike all the way home and slammed my way into the house. Excitedly, I asked my dad how he liked the game. "Yes," dad said, "it was pretty good. But who was that little guy who got the hit late in the game and got Eddie to third?"

Fame seems to go faster than it comes.

(Author's Note: I've since learned that my hit was not during the championship game. However, I'm leaving this episode as written; being a hero comes so seldom to the average Joe. It did happen the way I tell it but in another game. So it wasn't a big miracle but all those years I thought it was. My memory was a foul ball.)

Chapter 7

Oh, it was a wondrous time. We roamed freely for hours a day with just a break for lunch (my special delight was peanut butter and mustard sandwiches). Fat never had time to take hold; we outran it.

Contrary to the sentiments of today's heavily structured safety programs for kids, it was not a miracle that few of us got hurt. We just played so hard we had enough calluses padding our extremities that the slings and arrows of life simply bounced off. Kids ran loose and weren't limited by the town boundaries. We played out every day it wasn't blizzarding and only came in when it got too dark to play kick the can, a game I loved.

We had little reason to worry. There were no perverts around to worry mom. They weren't allowed to roam free as so many are today, but that's another story and maybe those today that are mentally disturbed will by another miracle be taken care of. But back then the bad guys didn't make themselves nuisances. Somebody might've strung 'em up.

Times were indeed more relaxed. Sure, we had a world war raging and polio was making its way into our lives. We did what kids do, though. We lived life every day and the only politically correct speech we knew was the Pledge of Allegiance. We were naïve in our naiveté. We didn't have new math, which some years later was dropped on kids who were supposed to understand what a physicist wrote in the1960s: The new math answer was *a member of the set which is the intersection of the set of those numbers which is larger than six and the set of numbers which are smaller than nine*. Some say the U.S. national debt exponentially grew from a new political viewpoint that believed new math would so confuse the voters.

Sensitivity training meant you didn't rat out your brother because you knew he'd get even.

Almost every boy had a dog, or at least the family did. I had Dandy, a mutt of indeterminate breed. Mutts or mongrels are said to be a lot smarter than the "breeds." Mutts have little to be proud of except their intellect, which is often awesome. They are independent, free and always exploring. They have no shame unless their master or mistress points it out.

Sort of like Americans. I've often thought that America is a mongrel nation. We come from so many backgrounds and ancestries we aren't saddled with protocols and royal vices. We just naturally go our own way and surmount the world and its challenges as need be. Maybe that's what makes America so great. I'm proud of my "mixed breed."

Anyway, Dandy didn't need a master. Oh, he tolerated me because he loved me. Dogs are like that. Cats…? They're okay, but it is a scientifically unverified fact: Cats expect love as their due and only reciprocate when they're hungry, cold or want petting.

Dandy escorted me on my downtown paper route. In fact, he knew the route as well as I and would lots of times wander off on his own, only to meet me four or five minutes later at another part of the route.

If I would go in one door of an office or apartment house, he might come with me or just meet me at the other door. He was never late. The only time we had any trouble was when a grumpy apartment manager cussed us out and told me never to bring that danged dog in there again. We started a chagrined retreat and for the one and only time, Dandy lifted his leg and anointed a hall corner. Now, thinking back on it, I don't think Dandy ever went there again. Guess he sensed he wasn't welcome.

Dandy died while I was in the Air Force. Word around town was he just wore himself out chasing cars and lady dogs. 'Nfact, just before he died, Loveland police officer Shorty Gates called the family. Dandy was collapsed on the other side of town. Just like any other pursuer of the delights offered by the opposite sex, he just plain ran out of gas and couldn't get home. My younger brother took the Radio Flyer wagon and pulled the old gay blade home.

I don't remember how old Dandy was when he died, but when he was younger I did keep track of his automobile hits. He also loved to chase rabbits just as much as cars and the last time I checked, he'd been hit by six cars, one motorcycle and one car he'd hit on his own. That particular adventure happened when he flushed some rabbits from the back lot. He was gaining on one that was heading for the street. The rabbit judged right and ran in front of a car, missing it by about two feet. Dandy couldn't stop and Whump! He caved in the right front passenger door. He was stunned but I didn't dare go to his aid. I was afraid I'd have to pay for that mashed-in door. After a few minutes, he got to his feet and staggered home, not much worse for wear.

I felt his loss even as far away as 3,000 miles. I experienced a sense that I'd lost at least a small miracle. Not often do we encounter unlimited love here in the secular world.

Chapter 8

As Boy Scouts, though sort of blasé about tying knots, I don't remember whether any of us made Tenderfoot or won any merit badges in those days, but that wasn't the point.

We'd tell ghost stories and sometimes even talk about what we were gonna be if we ever grew up, which didn't take much imagination. It was either college, the military or pumping gas at the local station run by an uncle or dad's friend. Weren't no CSAP tests and "no child left behind" was not yet a gleam in some politician's eye. We were all behind which made us equals and we didn't have much else with which to compare.

One miracle I don't believe happened then or in later years but even now befogs men; understanding that girls are different. Junior high was about the time when we began to notice girls were strange. Not just classmates who couldn't throw a ball for beans. But they were wittingly taking on an aura that somehow resembled yesterday's fascination with our baseball bat. To a young lad, bats were all different when you looked closely and discovered that each one had its own shape; a different curve, don't you know. Some even seemed to have a distinctive "grain." A girl's pert smile, cute nose or whatever began to take on yesterday's appeal for hitting a single.

One day, a boy would just wake up and learn that girls actually had something to say that, even if a guy figured on it awhile, it took a new kind of coping to understand, a skill with which we were anemic. Like, "Henry, if you don't quit teasing me, I'm going to kiss you!" Now if there weren't a lot of your buddies close by, you just had to stop and consider a bit. If the guys were within earshot, you were off the hook because you'd be so busy trying to slough off their teasing. But, that night you thought about it, yes you did.

The notion of actually kissing a girl, though, came later, after some lingering study, maybe a mushy scene in a movie western. Or an astonishingly gross exhibition by some adults. The first time I realized that real people did that a whole lot, kiss, was when a bunch of us were walking to school. All of a sudden a car screeched to a halt just a bit ahead of us. This soldier, just getting home from World War II, jumped out. Had an olive drab duffle bag over his shoulder which he flang clear up into the front porch bushes. At that moment his wife busted out the front door, ran to the soldier and hung a kiss on him that that looked like it was going to go on until the Second Coming. Leslie, one of the more suave junior highers, remarked: "Man, if he don't let up on her, he's gonna have three kids by Thursday.

The older girls ooohed and ahhhed all the way to school. The older guys just sorta grinned and looked at each other in an inconclusive way. Us youngin's just stared at the show until we were a half block away and I s'pose we were wondering, "What in the world were they thinking, acting like that so early in the morning?"

A few weeks later, I was playing with my friend, Oriel, a little girl from across the street. I guess we were both the same age, six or so, and I got to wondering about that soldier and his wife making such a spectacle of themselves that day. What's this kissin' stuff all about, anyway? The only way to find out, I did. I grabbed Oriel by the shoulders and pulled her to me. What I hadn't considered was that she had a runny nose that day and all I got was a mouthful of snot.

Well, now, I'm thinking, I must be doing something wrong. I didn't kiss another girl for ten long years—and she was the one that initiated it. Then I had the revelation: "So that's how it's done" and from then on I did.

Growing up wasn't so hard until you crossed that deep, muddy river with girls. But it was just gawd-awful confusing after fording. There was no government blessed sex education in those days. You learned the way you learned and sometimes it was miss *and* hit! One day, Eddie and I were down at the swimming hole, swinging on this old rope tied high in a cottonwood tree and splattering ourselves into the Big Thompson River. A friend, Joe, I think, joined us. Joe had older brothers who were, uh, experienced.

We swung and dropped until we got tired and laid on the river bank watching the clouds go by. Then, without so much as a preamble (if he'd thought about it, he probably would've been too embarrassed to ask), Eddie turned to Joe and asked, "What is it about girls?"

Joe thought about it for a long time and then offered this pearl. "Well, thing about it is, there's two special places on a girl. All you gotta do is figger out which one makes her twitch." It was several years later that Eddie and I finally came to understand what Joe had taught us: Women are just different. That was sex education in the Fifties.

Chapter 9

Everyone pitched in to help the war effort once it did break out. As kids, we took part in paper drives and gathered scrap metal for the war effort. Once, The First Baptist Youth Fellowship group decided we would rent ourselves out as part of a fundraiser. Figuring on cutting lawns and whitewashing fences or something thereabouts, we put ourselves up for auction, I think to raise money for more bullets. It was a most unpleasant experience.

One of the congregation was a chicken farmer, name of Branson. A lot of the young men had been called to duty and hired help was getting sparse. Branson was a member of the church so he put in the first bid. He proposed six of us clean his chicken house. Lots of folks raised chickens in those days but farm kids were in the minority at Sunday School. Those kids did not volunteer for the chicken cleanup.

The rest of us didn't wonder too much about why the farm kids went after "city" jobs. When us city slickers got to the farm, we found what probably would have vexated even the future Col. Saunders to the point of rewriting his business plan.

That bloody chicken house seemed a block long and when we went inside, a couple classmates puked. And maybe for the first time we realized that chickens not only lay eggs, they poop. A lot! Beneath those perches was a layer of undiluted chicken manure as deep as a Colorado January snowfall.

So the non-pukers were given a scoop shovel, which left the pukers to do the outside piling while us others began what later was known as the Great Junior High Poop Penance. It was smelly, oh, was it putrid. In my seventy-five-plus years the only thing I've experienced that was that pungent was a bowl of kimchi, a famous Korean epicurean delight that, if you are in a coma, is edible.

By taking turns and coming out to suck air about every ten minutes, we got her cleaned but it was several years before I could eat chicken in any form without getting all balled up inside. (Years, later one of our on-par-with-impossible-to-emulate sales ladies at the Walter Publishing Company newspapers told us about her growing-up days. When she'd get frustrated with her parents' unreasonableness, she'd go out and kick a chicken. "It makes a most satisfying thunk, one, you know, you'd never experience after kicking one of your parents.")

I have not tried it but just the thought of kicking one of those blasted flightless, only-useful-for-target-practice birds makes me quiver. Still can't eat eggs.

We didn't have gang members recruiting us and drugs were sold only at drug stores. Polio was on the wane and we were too timorous to try to buy cigarettes. Once again, it was that specter of "What if they call dad to see if I'm old enough?" In those days, dads weren't the boobs and klutzes we see today on TV. Somehow Dads most often learned what was going on and what to do about it when things needed some doing about. The modern awful, hurtful, growth-defying "time out" would've made the juvenile delinquents of the day howl with laughter. Dads knew how to gain and keep our attention: They whupped our butts behind the barn or garage. I don't remember my dad doing that, though. He had this look that made you feel residual pain.

I also can't recall anyone who was "grounded." Maybe some of the girls, but in those halcyon "Tom Sawyer" days, grounding a boy meant spading the garden in the spring or digging out dandelions in the front yard or cutting weeds in the orchard. I admit some of us were more "well-grounded" than others, depending on what kind of day dad had at work.

Speaking of dads, in those days fooling around was, uh, a more thought provoking subject, you might say. Like "What have I gone and done?" For girls, aid to dependent children wasn't even in our community language.

Most dads had shotguns and the boys knew it. Sure, a few young couples got in trouble, like in the family way, but if the boy didn't lean toward voluntary matrimony, he was given a choice: Either join the Navy or buy a ring and promise to be a good husband and daddy.

In junior high, boys were still afraid of girls. I don't know why except, being laughed at by a girl was worse than diarrhea. Boys didn't understand girls in those days any more than today and future male archeologists will still be asking the same question: "What did I say?" One difference I noted was that girls always carried home a big armload of books? Were they reading them or what? We didn't question it much. After all, girls were just… inconclusive?

As a matter of fact, though, it was a girl that maybe sowed the seed of another miracle. Although she didn't know it, she was responsible for my discovering one of the true loves of my life. Back about third grade I fell in love with singing through one of the Seven Deadly Sins: Envy. The girl next door was chosen to sing in the city-wide spring concert with kids from all three grade schools. I didn't because I was pretty sure boys were sissies if they didn't sing bass like their dads. So, since I couldn't—sing bass—I didn't.

Well, when LaVon was chosen to be part of that elite group of young vocalists, I was so jealous I would've cried—except dad might've caught me. And the odd thing was I didn't really like her. But for some reason I determined—one of the few times I planned anything—to learn how to sing before next year's concert.

That summer I practiced singing. I even learned a little yodeling by listening to cowboy Red Smith on the radio every morning before school. I didn't know until years later that all the neighbors began to wonder if my mom was beating the snot out of me. But warble I did. And when the next year's concert rolled around, ol' Hank was up there with them, singing his heart out. (I wanted to yodel but the choir director felt I'd be a bigger help if I sang tenor.)

I discovered I loved to sing. It was fun. I mingled well with music. And, even though I didn't realize it yet, it was a marvelous stress reducer. I'm sure it changed my life in the coming years. To make my harmonious life richer, I found I had perfect pitch and as I grew older and sang in a quartet, we didn't need a pitch pipe. I just hummed the first note and off we went.

I also practiced enough that I could sing about two and a half octaves. For those who don't experience the joy of singing, that's pretty good. I must say here that some of the most interesting and happy people are singers; not all great, as I demonstrated and for the most part, when amateurs sing there just isn't any fussing about being flat or sharp—for the most part.

I sang though grade school, junior high, high school and for forty-seven years in my church choir.

I'm a beer baritone (crooner Dean Martin, by contrast, was a whiskey baritone of finer quality), but I sing tenor at church because there ain't nobody else will sing tenor. And, in that time I also wrote and performed two love songs to Carolyn. I bought a bass ukulele—I found my fingers were too short for a six-string guitar—and taught myself to play it just for Carolyn. And as I thought about it in later years, if I'd had my druthers, I might have become a Broadway composer. Yes, music can do that to a person, change their outlook on life. I will always be thankful, first for LaVon's unconscious push and for God giving me just enough voice to be part of a wonderful group of people.

When I got to junior high, I became part of a trio that went around to other schools and "old" ladies' tea parties singing "Chattanooga Shoe Shine Boy." That was the "boogy woogie boy" who could fan the air with his shoeshine rag with a hippity hop hoppity hip. That was my part. Got so wrapped up in all that singing, a buddy and I wrote a minstrel show and the teacher agreed to put it on for a school assembly. Naturally, we wrote ourselves in as the "end men," the guys who got to tell the jokes.

We worked long hours writing the show. Then, just about the time of dress rehearsal, we were both kicked out of the show. We were devastated and more than somewhat mystified by the teacher's hasty action. Seems we were kidding around during practice and stuck our tongues out at each other. Bang! We were has-beens.

We later learned that the teacher had come to this conclusion that tongues sticking out meant something dirty. We didn't know that and for a couple weeks we were "puberly" perplexed. In the 50s teachers had authority and they used it, seldom abused it. But we knew, right or wrong, the teacher was the final authority. Our folks said so.

Discovery that I could and that I did enjoy singing to my mind will always be a miracle. Fifty years later, I'm still recalling incidents of the past that are making my Golden Years the best part of my life.

Yet, for some reason, boys don't sing as much today. They listen to something called Rap, a musical genre that would only thrill Thumper, the rabbit. I'm afraid the younger generation will never experience the thrill of making their own music. Or if they do, you won't hear 'em because the amplification is so loud. Girls? It may be that they've been making their own music since Eve hummed her siren song to Adam. A friend once told me God put girls here to make music to a boy's (man's) heart and I've seldom had reason to doubt my friend's veracity.

Chapter 10

The war was over. New cars (the war precluded manufacturing anything but jeeps and tanks) were again seen on the streets. All kinds of new fangled gadgets were being invented and sold that hadn't been available for years. John Q. Public soon would need more automobile horsepower, more oil and, of course, that made for more sales tax revenue for the government.

It was a wonderful time, what with ice boxes being replaced by fridges and restaurants you could actually drive up to and they'd send these cute girls in short skirts coming out to be your waitress. It seemed as if the newly-supplied-with-materials inventers and entrepreneurs were going to make a brand new world from the shambles we'd made of it through two world wars in less than two generations.

Graduation from grade school and then from junior high was anti-climatic. Other than some new challenges such as trying to visualize ourselves as "upper classmen," there were no celebrations. Our learning schedule seemed to speed up, though. Our seventh grade science teacher was a piece of work. Had some very firm notions, one being if you chewed on your pencil, he took it, rolled it under his shoe on the floor and then dared you to chew on it since now it was loaded with germs—or so he said. Some of the guys dared—puberty breeds pluck as well as pangs of uncertainty—and got Ds for the semester but they proved they wouldn't die the horrible death ol' Frank claimed they would. I didn't. My pencils were pure the whole class because I wasn't all that sure the old fellow didn't know something about hygiene. (I later learned he didn't care much about hygiene).

He set up an experiment to prove there is no such thing as a vacuum. He was a lousy teacher. He didn't even realize that there were four or five of us guys sitting right in front of him that were living proof of its existence. He passed most all of us anyway, when we started asking questions he didn't want to contend with the next year.

Leaving junior high meant you traveled about 10 feet to the east and Voila! You were in high school. The main difference, as I recall, was there was a little hump in the floor of about two inches, which raised the high school to a level us angst-ridden ninth graders had only feared attaining. But it also was a source of pride in our parents. Many of them, unfortunately, never made it that far in their school days.

We learned early on about hierarchy, too, from the new sophomores who just last spring had been our friends but now let us know they were superior. I've noticed throughout life there is always a "sophomore" ahead of you, no matter how successful or rich you become. Even the President of the United States has a boss. He just doesn't acknowledge who we are these days.

We had more fun then. At least I did. I had become the class clown, later graduating into jerkism 101 in senior high. At my 50th high school class reunion, a lady who I'd once had a crush on said—gently of course, "You were a mess in high school, Hank." Maybe so, but I was enjoying myself. I still clown around a bit, but I'm more demure since I got great grandchildren.

All the boys wore Levis and every now and then clean white t-shirts. The girls, I think, wore skirts and bobby socks, but at that age most boys just noticed the girls' calves and followed them to catch a glimpse if they happened to walk with the sun at their back. That, by the way, was when I learned boys could still be boys—and weren't sent to sensitivity training for drooling. There were just some things that all the learning in the world couldn't improve upon and a shapely silhouette in a skirt being exploited by God's beautiful sunset was one.

We had the typical cliques, you know, the royalty and the "others." I believe I was right between uninvited and untouchable but I never knew which. I went my merry way, albeit secretly yearning to be a "socialite." However, I'll swear to a Supreme Court Justice (that's as high as our diversified society allows anymore) I would never have made it to young adulthood had I deigned to "discover" who I really was. As it was, I never experienced depression until I received my first 1040 tax form.

Grades weren't as decisive in those secondary school days. A "C" was good because that was average and most of us were average, which meant we didn't spend every waking moment worrying about which elite university we would not be admitted to. I did get one A before I graduated. But I had to (zounds!) work for it. My junior year I was supposed to do a notebook for English. I did and I thought it was perfect. The teacher, Miz Hook, didn't. I said it was. She said it wasn't. I avowed I deserved an A. She said I'd probably never work hard enough to get an A in anything but playing dumb. So I bet her she'd end up giving me an A by the end of the semester. Got my A and then went back to working just enough for Cs.

Actually, I may have gotten another A in Home and Family Living. I was told by some ladies at our 50th reunion that I had turned in a theme assignment that had very little to do with the instructions Mrs. Worden gave. But I had written around it so assiduously, she thought my effort to avoid work deserved proper recognition.

You'd think I'd remember something as rare as that but I was probably arguing with Miz Worden—my favorite sport—about whether it should be called a pot holder or a pot rag. She didn't like "rag" much. I quickly learned it seemed a little hickish to her, which gave me a chance to practice my debating skills. Deep down, I think I would have loved her except I had a crush on her daughter. A man can handle only so much good fortune before his intentions become a bit confusing—to himself.

Some, but not many, of the future Joe and Jill College kids' folks had diligently put away a little stash for higher education. In those days, nearby colleges were on the quarter system and cost about $64 in tuition and $20 for used books. You lived at home or paid about five bucks a week to sleep in somebody's crawl space. College was affordable for everyone unless you wanted that Corvette before you were educated enough to earn it instead of steal it. That, of course, applies only if you don't decide to go into politics. There, it seems, you indeed can have your Corvette long before you earn it.

I wasn't planning to attend college, especially after mom told me I wasn't smart enough, so don't waste the professors' time. She advised me to go into the Air Force for four years while some of my buddies were evading the draft by conscientiously learning about the world through education and I was off fighting the wars from my U.S. Air Force administrative desk. (Mom, I still love you and I forgive you for saving me from all that college partying.)

The rest of the guys became GIs—the Universal Military Training was still in effect. The girls... Well, they went into nursing and teaching or got jobs in the local stores or whatever was available. My next oldest sister became the town librarian assistant until she got married to Jon, a farmer from the next town of Berthoud.

After the military or the drudgery of a civilian job, some of us caught on and went to college anyway.

I think our parents' advice was well meant when they discouraged going to college. They had been through some tough times and only wanted us to get a job and earn a paycheck. However, at high school graduation time, we were so poor we didn't realize poverty was curable. We found out soon enough that many or most of us, with the aid of some small miracles—and some midsized—did pretty well in this country of unlimited opportunity. Some didn't because they limited their opportunities by believing the life they'd known was as good as it was going to get.

God was with us fortunate few. But—by the grace of God—and thank you, America, almost all my class of 55 seemed to prosper through the years, even those sans that high powered college degree.

Chapter 11

I didn't notice any miracles in my high school days but I'm sure they were there. Because things did happen that now I recollect upon could have been miracles, albeit small ones. (Is it possible that a little miracle is as important as a big one? Very likely. The human mind works against us about as often as it works for us.)

I remember a day when my "earned" self-esteem was at a low pitch. Somewhere around sixteen or so I was driving my old 1937 Chevrolet through town that seemed to be deserted. Of course, it wasn't, but those other people just didn't connect with me, or vice versa. Anyway, I got to a busy intersection. There were, it seemed, fifty or more cars each way on the cross street, or at least as far as I could see in each direction. I stopped at the red light and waited. And while I was waiting, I was daydreaming and feeling a little sorry for myself.

Then a thought bounced off my thinking cap (a third grade teacher always advised us to "put on your thinking caps..." before we started a new lesson). Dumb as it sounds, I right then and there at that stoplight realized I was someone important. The light changed and since I was the only vehicle waiting at that particular intersection, it seemed to me that I had the power. I, Hank, could stop a hundred other people all by myself. Me! All those hundred or so drivers had to stop just for me!

Nutty or not, from that day forward I could at least pretend I was somebody because the world (at least at that intersection) had to acknowledge me. Dumb idea? Maybe, but sometimes that's all it takes to perk you up and make you think a bit more clearly. I don't know where that silly idea came from, but it worked for me and I still believe the Holy Spirit gave me a nudge.

So go out and stop traffic the next time you're feeling low.

Except it made me think I was maybe not so unimportant. Maybe that's where I started thinking about more than what I could see and feel or taste. I was part of life and part of many other lives. Why should I keep telling myself I was "nuthin'?" That led to other wool gathering sessions and, I think, enhanced the vague idea of miracles in my life.

Sure, there were times when we (I) thought our world was ended. Like not getting a part in the junior play because a guy I didn't like got the part and I just knew my tryout would be emotionally worthy even if he did already know his lines. I was better for the part!

Or learning that your best friend now had a girl and you had been cut loose to make your own lonely way up the river of life.

Rambling thoughts aside, I did experience a "delayed" miracle that forty years later kept me from working too hard and illuminated a goal in life. I think it was my sophomore year when an English teacher gave us an assignment to write a letter to a friend. Aw, what the heck, I thought, she can't be too serious about this. No worry. I scribbled out my letter that night and turned it in next day.

A couple days later, the teacher surprised me. She read my letter to Pauli to the class, laughing all the way through. I was embarrassed to be singled out in front of the whole class; I thought she was making fun of me. The class laughed some, (as the class clown, they were used to me, I guess), but after class, Ms. Houseman asked me to stay a minute. Then she said, "Hank, you have a real talent. You should pursue a writing career."

Sure, and I probably could be a B-29 bomber pilot if I could have reached the pedals, I thought as I walked out of class and forgot about it for two score years, until I launched a newspaper. More about that later.

I think we learned to cope well, us fifties scamps and fillies. There was none of this philosophy of "don't worry, someone will be there for you"—usually a government agency just bursting to make you a "free" slave beholden to handouts. I busted out with that C average. In fact, I think, other than those frivolous As, I got all Cs and maybe a D in algebra. Algebra bored me then and later I realized I should have paid more attention. The value of X has taken on more importance over the years and now, what with Congress using up all that ink for paper XXs to make a1950s X the same as a 2012 XXXXXXs. I'm not sure we can afford another X.

Chapter 12

Mostly high school was my time to wander in a semi-coma and maybe learn a little English Lit or wrestle a bit with some other sweaty guy trying to paste me to a canvas mat when I had gotten careless and missed my "grabba holt." And a time of senior pictures and the prom and then…GRADUATION. May 1955.

Then came the morning after. The first day of the rest of my life. I awakened and realized I didn't have any plans for today—or any future day. And I'm asking, "Oh my God. What have I gone and done? I'm a graduate and I don't even have street smarts! What do I do now? What do I know? If

I get a job I'll have to work Saturdays. And all summer. And maybe forever! Woe upon me.

I'd taken the school IQ test. The only thing it had told me was that I could be an entrepreneur: I could flush with either hand. Trouble was I didn't know what an entrepreneur was supposed to flush.

Some called it dismissing puberty, a necessary requisite for facing maturity, a thing I knew not enough about because, if it was ever explored in class, I must have been asleep. And, too, maturity doesn't always follow on the heels of puberty. The 1960s Haight-Ashbury hippies demonstrated that exceedingly well.

Now that I think back on it, 1955 was about the time I and a lot of my contemporaries quit enjoying music. Somehow we lost our rhythm and didn't dig the beat. There was that guy name of Elvis who didn't necessarily sing; he twitched, with gyrations we were not yet into. We were shocked to learn that unsophisticated rhythm was to be the beat for the next fifty years. Then, too, there were those Beatles guys whom we couldn't understand because they were beat, beat, beating so fast and speaking a language few of us had bothered to learn well. We were left in the gloaming with our memories of Johnnie Ray singing "The Little White Cloud That Cried."

Which is probably why a whole generation lost interest in pop music? And why so many of the Class of 55 came to like classical, jazz, bluegrass, Christian, western, rhythm and blues, country music… I mean, c'mon, when we were growing up we had classics like "That's How a Heartache Begins," and other songs like "Mule Train," "Sam's Song," like that, you know, was music for true connoisseurs such as we.

In the middle 50s, there was this thing called "Duty to God and Country—Hup!" for guys like me that started planning their future the day after it arrived. It was called the Draft. If you didn't sign up voluntarily before your number came up, you would be firmly invited to come anyway and you wouldn't get your choice of assignments. That was not a good thing; you might be trained as a Military Policeman and I don't think they would have found a Billy club small enough for my hand.

Funny thing happened on the way to the draft board. Another little miracle?

I was too small to be a Marine. My 20/400 vision allowed that I wasn't going to be a sailor.

The swabbie just laughed, said I wouldn't be able to find the ocean, let alone float on it.

The army recruiter obviously felt I was benighted (Took me twenty years to finally look up that word. Only thing I can figure is I had small feet.) or I wouldn't be trying to voluntarily enlist in the infantry. The Coast Guard? The recruiter just shook his head; said I was too short to see over the mainmast.

Flummoxed, I was walking toward the door, my head down, my angst growing, my butt dragging. It was then I heard this "Off We Go!" sorta voice saying, "Young man. C'mere." And I ended up "fighting the wars" by flying an Olivetti typewriter for four years in the almost new USAF. I didn't carry an M1. I didn't sail away to glory. I learned to type. Hoo Ah. My way of looking at it is had I gotten my choice of services, I might have become a hero leaving the possibility of reenlistment out of false pride—and heroes are always given the tough jobs.

As it turned out my unheroic four years under the military command system left me with a new respect for the democratic way of life. The military, though, for obvious reasons demonstrated quite clearly that freedom was only for those we were protecting, not us GIs. Somehow I got to missing choices, like food, job, abode and hair style.

And so I ended up defending my country with Gen. Curtis LeMay's Strategic Air Command. The only miracle here, I guess, would be that I didn't wound anyone by flipping my typewriter platen too aggressively.

I proved to be an average GI except, in 1955-59 I wasn't a "real" GI. I learned four years later at my discharge that those benefits such as mustering out pay, college, GI home financing weren't available to my era. The government had stopped the GI bill just before I volunteered. It was later renewed and vets in my generation did get a belated gift of benefits.

The military life was fun when we learned the art of marching as syncopated warriors. I was good! Some of my compatriots believed I greased the inside of my shoes, I was so smooth. I could do a TO THE REAR, HARCH! better than anybody but the Filipinos, who made up a large part of our training population at that time. Those Filipinos were uncanny. They could do a left oblique on ice and never miss a beat.

The problem was, in the stateside domesticated parade strut, there were all these tall guys. So when we'd line up for a parade, there was this rule that said if the man in front of you was shorter, take a step forward. I always ended up in the last rank and you know what they did? They told the last rank to "Fall Out!"

I never got to march in front of an admiring audience but I've always known I was an airman who was perfectly capable of doing a "Right Oblique About Face" without touching my feet to the ground while tying my brogans. Now it may be that little slight by the drill sergeants slanted me away from becoming a military hero even though there was no war to fight in those days. I still haven't completely forgiven the USAF for that disgusting example of squirt discrimination.

I served two years at Fairchild Air Force Base near Spokane, Washington. I did okay; made Airman of the Month once, possibly because I had learned to type official orders, and got a free weekend at the fine Davenport Hotel in downtown Spokane, Washington.

My-Air-Force-veteran older brothers had advised me on how to survive the military. One thing I was told—and totally ignored—was "Never turn your back on the Air Force Personnel Department." Cavalierly ignoring the vets, I decided one year to take my allotted 30-day leave. Not a good idea. When I returned to duty, I learned I was on a shipment to "Airman's Paradise," Thule Air Force Base, Greenland. We were told by our superiors Thule was about five hundred miles from the North Pole. That was when I really knew there was no Santa; even USAF warplanes fully equipped with RADAR had a tough time getting airborne. Rudolf, my foot!

Thule supported a program called the "The Dew Line." The U.S. had set up missile sites around the world and needed someone to watch when the Russians launched their ballistic missiles to wipe out Milwaukee or maybe even Loveland. I was personally chosen by one of the most effective Generals the USAF ever had. I, A/1C Henry A. Walter, AF serial #17443438, was to shout out *Lookout below!* if the Russians did pull the trigger so that all the rest of you guys back in the states could duck. We were anointed as official members of the "Knights of the Blue Nose" and we were ready—mostly since there was no way out of Thule until your time had come, one way or t'other.

At least we weren't lying in frozen foxholes. We had great chow halls and clubs, even a gym and a movie theater showing first run movies back in

'58 and '59. Though after seeing the second, third and… western at Thule, we sorta lost interest. See, Hollywood at that time was using one scenery set in New Mexico or Arizona for every western and it took away some of the realism watching different cowboy heroes charge across that same bridge to rescue a different heroine each time the Indians retook either the Mexican village or the Texas town. The best way to keep track was to watch which side of the bridge the bad guys were coming from.

It's likely John Wayne didn't have to memorize too many lines. He just turned one way or the other and shot the villains crossing that same bridge, time after time.

Chapter 13

Yessir, Thule could be a trial and I suspected so my very first day. I walked into the barracks and noticed all these short-timers watching TV—but not really. When another airman walked over and turned the TV *on*, no one seemed to notice or care. I knew it was gonna be a really long year.

Thule gave me a glimpse of the miracles the U.S, military had accomplished during World War II and the post war period. There were so many things invented during those dark times, the American public was almost overwhelmed trying to buy it all. Of course not all those futuristic products were what one would call miraculous.

Some were jury-rigged conglomerates of old steel and ingenuity.

Although we first had a session on how to close those double doors on the reversed barracks—like a deep freeze only heated inside—and what would happen to you if you were in a hurry to thaw your butt and left one door open. You were thrown outside for as many times as it took to learn that blue was not an airman's favorite color.

Another wonderful improvement over WW II was the *Thule Toilet* instead of the latrine pit. It was made by attaching a 1920s toilet bowl with a 1934 Ford shift lever. Now there was a contraption never to earn the designation of miracle. The highlight of our orientation was learning how to flush the danged thing. Not a simple task. By way of explanation, there is no water in Thule except what is trucked in from the ice cap. This valuable commodity was then pumped into a holding tank and used for washing, tooth brushing, etc. From there it was speed-shifted into a second tank where it was recycled as "toilet flush." It was aromatically an attention getter, but harmless if you carefully paid attention *before* exposing your tender, uh, parts to it.

If you didn't shift quickly, it became a potential Dante's Loo.

If you learned the ropes and held your breath, you could experience relief with relative ease. If you didn't catch on the by the second attempt, you prayed for constipation. Leaving out the more mundane details, quick reaction with some adroitness which, if you did it right, all turned out well.

Slow learners would find themselves spat upon and the front of their uniform dankly darkened by a cold blast of awful cold and black water that could be alleviated only by multiple cleanings at the base laundry. But that wasn't the worst. I later learned there are worse situations. I overslept one too many times and got the grand prize for dawdling in the Arctic.

That third water tank, remember, was filled with really awful water left after us humans had polluted. And it dripped and it froze right outside the barracks forming a pyramid about five foot high. Every two weeks or so a truck came around and emptied "Dante's chamber pot" which by now had built up to a brownish-green sorta icy hill. And somebody then had to use a large ice pick to chip away ugly muck. This was done by errant airmen such as I. The little ice chips would fly, landing in your hair and fur collar. It really was such a waste.

The coup de grace was a surprise later when you were finished whittling the thing down to a size you could heave in the truck and went into the barracks to get warm. The coat thawed. The little chips became a highly relevant part of civil dissonance among your choking peers. There was no way to clean it and thusly you, my dear airman, became the object of ribald jokes and some serious threats. The whole barracks smelled of your ineptness and you were an untouchable, condemned to stay in your room with the door securely closed until you could take your parka to the base laundry. A task not always immediately accomplished due to inclement weather much of the time.

I never overslept again until college. Still, potty training did help break up a boring day in Airman's Paradise, where there are two seasons: Daylight, cold; nighttime, dark and cold.

One odd thing did happen—which gave me my first inkling miracles do exist. It occurred when a couple buddies and I were humping it back to the barracks after a movie. They were hometown friends and were chatting about their love life before they enlisted. They were trying to remember a girl's name. Suddenly I knew it was "Gloria." The talk went on for a few minutes as I tried to screw up the courage speak out. Before I could get up the nerve, one of my fellow airmen burst out: "Gloria! I remember now."

I knew! I never told them but it was a sure thing in my mind. Later in life, as I was trying to decipher what that "Heaven's Better" message, I recalled "Gloria." There are some things going on with humans we just don't understand. If the mind can clutch a name from the ether, why would anyone doubt a message from God? I think maybe we work too hard at doubting our own miracle—our mind.

There were other diversions, however, that kept us awake at night. It was called KP. That's kitchen police for those who care. First, you had to get up early enough to get to the assigned chow hall before the earliest hungry troopers. KP was slave labor in the chow halls where you learned you were less than a poorly trained beast of burden. We were waiters, cooks' helpers, pot washers, kings of the garbage dock…fun things a non-entity would enjoy.

I was assigned to the officers' mess in Thule and I got lucky. My first duty was to keep the garbage dock ready for pickup. I had already learned in boot camp that if you were discovered goofing off on KP, you earned yourself a little extra duty, like folding napkins while the other simians took their break.

So after the first truck had emptied the garbage cans, I looked around for a place to hide. The dock was pretty nude, peopled only by muckily crusted cans and it was my job to make them militarily correct. I'm standing there with the hot water hose in my hand wondering how to make myself as innocuous as a cockroach, spraying the water on those smelly cans to keep warm. I kept spraying and before long had the dock clean as a whistle—after I'd washed away items that made me want to puke. At that moment, the head cook came to see if I was worthy of my three stripes and doing my part to save humanity from the Evil Empire.

He was so surprised and pleased, I got off two hours earlier than the other KPs and I later learned he had requested me for KP when my next turn came around. Miracle? No, I was just cold. After that I was permanently on the garbage dock (little work to do if you kept the warm nozzle handy) because, as the cook/sergeant later told me, I was the only one who took initiative and made the garbage dock a place he was proud to show to the base commander if the commander ever wanted to inspect the garbage dock.

Today's Air Force is a bit different from fifty years ago. Had I experienced the Flyboy world of today, I might have remained a long-termer. The "Off We Go" airmen today exhibit pride and mastery of mission not even dreamed of in 1947-59.

And so the USAF bade goodbye to A/1C Henry A. Walter by giving me a plane ticket home to Colorado. They also paid me for my accrued leave, which was about 30 days pay. And you know, I was so grateful I didn't waste a minute before buying some really tacky civilian clothes on the way to the airport.

Chapter 14

Mom had been right about my not being ready for college. If truth be known, four years after high school, I still was not ready for any known-to-a-dreamer vocational direction. But I'd been encouraged to pursue an educational degree of some kind and maybe become a teacher of young minds so I gave it a shot. I enrolled at the fine old revered Colorado State College of Education (even remembering that long name planted some misgivings in my memory skill) as a first quarter freshman. On the spur of the moment—and at the insistence of a counselor who said if I didn't make up my mind soon, I'd be the oldest freshman in the history of higher elucidation—I signed up for business education courses.

Little mistake. The only business experience I'd had were several schemes running from about fifth grade to high school, none of which ever got off the ground. One I remember was when a buddy and I decided to buy some hand-held fishnets and sweep up golden profits from a bridge over the Big Thompson River that ran through Loveland. Mom squashed that venture immediately. It was illegal, she said. I didn't know what "illegal" meant but I decided to obey since she was getting to the point of giving a good switching.

Next was a deal to run a bicycle repair shop when I was a freshman in high school. Needed a partner for that though, not because I couldn't do it myself. I just needed a buddy to keep me company. In those days, I hated to be alone. I think at that time of my life I would have partnered with bin Laden just to have company. No partner was found, mostly because I was prepared only to pay about minimum wage (which didn't exist back then so it was pay what they'll take) to a helper. After all, it was my idea! As might have been predicted, there were no profits to split anyway.

It was at this stage of my life I hit the lowest level of my life. Proving what a low life I was and representing how far I had to go to becoming a good citizen and Christian. I was headed for a career as a burger flipper. I had married a fine girl early in my Air Force career. When I was discharged and before I quit college, I left her and our daughter. I had no reason other than my selfish longing for something else, my place in the sun, I guess. I have never really forgiven myself but God has. Otherwise, why would He waste time on such a bounder?

A second case of absolute comatose feelings for others, when I was at Thule, I took over a little coffee business being run by two other airmen. Unwittingly, I had given them some bad advice one day when the water supply had run out or frozen. I told them to melt some snow in the coffee pot and then make coffee.

The coffee pot burned up. I didn't apologize. No, without thinking, I called a buddy who hurried down to base supply with a new coffee pot and a supply of coffee, which I immediately brewed up and began selling for a nickel a cup. Didn't regret my scurrilous behavior for years but when I did, I could not believe I'd been so callous.

My first year at CSCE was pretty good. I took a test of some sort and came out as a first quarter sophomore before I'd finished my first freshman quarter. That was great. I'd save a lot of time getting that education degree. I didn't realize that by skipping three quarters, I would not be taking courses in the Humanities, etc. I've always regretted not taking those courses. I think I might have enjoyed getting fully educated.

As it turned out, I soon found I wasn't teacher material. First, I realized teaching business ed to high school kids had to be the most detantalizing direction I could have picked. I could type but when it came to learning to take shorthand I found it about as interesting as drinking fog. I couldn't teach kids to do that, at least not with a clear conscience.

Discouragement became quite evident when I met a couple guys who had been going to CSCE since before I graduated from elementary school back in 1946. I began to think education required more than sitting while listening to boring lectures. They were known as "professional students" and seemed to have no plans to graduate prior to Social Security or dementia; their calling seemed more in the nature of the wind in the willows—a whisper of uncertainty. Eternally attending lectures seemed a direct way to everlasting contemplation of the navel, which was just becoming popular in those days.

Another little miracle, I think, helped me decide to give up all the blessings of college might have afforded me. One of my first classes was Poly Sci. The only time I could enroll in the required course was during the lunch hour. Yeah, I loved lunch in those days and the professor probably is one of those most responsible for my later happiness in life. He flunked me for, I guess, disattendance or inattention. I consider it a miracle because if I'd been the least bit interested in political science, I might have—not saying I would—but might have gone into politics. God works in mysterious ways.

In the middle of my sophomore year, I threw in the towel. I was being force-fed accounting. It was very soon I recognized I was overmatched by accounting. I thought a debit was that little hole in the grass left by your golf club. Credit? That was something you could get from a banker if you didn't need it. I just didn't have the heart to keep wasting the professor's time.

I learned, though, I was not finished with accounting. The subject came back to haunt me years later after I had gone into business.

In 1996 a friend decided to teach me accounting. I said it would be a miracle if he succeeded. He said, "Don't worry a bit. I can teach anyone accounting. It's simple." He was a nice guy and I didn't want to hurt his feelings so I gave it my best shot.

We started with debits and credits. By the end of our session, I realized I was verging on a new lesson in my life. I remembered those days when I was pretending I could learn how to teach kids business. I think it would have been an unbelievable miracle had Al been successful.

Al went to his Maker just a few years later. I'm sure he went, understanding finally that he alone could *not* make a miracle happen. I hope he didn't have to explain too much because he really did try.

I wrote the following column partly as an elegy for Al but also to help me cope with my shortcomings and to assuage my mentor's shame at his failure to make me an asset for the newspaper.

More, though, I think the column set me on my journey to unearthing the truth of trusting God as my most dependable partner.

Once upon a tyme
It was a cold, drizzly morning that Memorial day. A sinister fog had wafted across the draw-bridge and settled over the computer screen.   I

whined as I tried to shake loose the mouse duct-taped to my right hand. My legs had long ago gone to sleep—the rope around my ankle securing me to the chair had cut off circulation even before I'd had my seven am cup of coffee.

"Forsooth, thou blasted evil spirit," I railed at Al the Champion, dark prince of Peachtree.

"Should I lose these bonds and attain yon delete key, thou pitiless auditor of agony, I'll send thee hieing to the spirits of hell!"

The Arithmetic Wizard of the Kingdom of Kalkulation rendered a wizened smile. "My lord of impotent illiteracy, would that thy impenetrable ignas fatuus be illumined. Humbly pray thee, boldly activate they cursor and thy publishing kingdom shall soar to the raptures of numerology and prodigious profitability. It is written," bespoke the Champion of Answerability.

I had been beguiled unto the Wizard's lair by his pledge of simplicity in my quest for utopian pelf. The Al of Champion had chastised me, pummeling my proud spirit with visions of poverty staining my royal robes. "We must be accountable," he regally proclaimed. "Crusade fearlessly, O you of modest wit."

What was bringing my karma lower than a dragon's belly was the Al's insistence that he could teach me the computer accounting system. I was leerful. Zounds! It sounded more difficult than locating Merlin's book of magic.

But I submitted my soul and allowed the Al to hurl his spearful will upon my writing spirit. "Lighten the darkness," I supplicated.

"Port and starboard," he pronounced.

"My karma is drowning and thy tongue wags nautical!" I sputtered.

"M'lord," the Al soothed, "thou must allow thy heart to dwell in harmony with the counting of the bean. Port and Starboard! I say."

"In the name of the blessed Arthur, elucidate, you maddened merchant of mathmatology."

"It becomes clear, O Lord of Imbecility, that thou must unlearn thy nugatory notions of tallying treasure. Port is left; starboard, right. Debits left; credits right. Onward, I say!"

"Too easy, I avowed, "else why doth the IRS, to expunge its rhetorical dissolution, accost the noble accountant?"

"Verily," the Al explained, "to the royal practitioner of polity propagation, left or right be only a state of mind brought forth on the occasion of posture-leaning at a two hundred dollar a plate fundraiser. T'is as good and evil; the

art of compromise. Alas, port and starboard may not be put to hazard. You milord, must believe that left and right truly exist in the nethermost. If it be not so, a beginning cannot end. Thus I proclaim."

I succumbed to his proclamation and again faced the dreaded screen. My trembling fore digit mashed the wretched mouse's left ear and behold, upon the screen emerged a number—a debit. It blinked its way to the left side. I punched the mouse's right ear and another sum wended its journey to the right. A credit thereby, embracing and balancing.

"That's it?" I was astonished.

"Just so" pontificated the AI, waving legerde-mainiacally through the ether.

Well, gadzooks, had I perceived the accounting so pliant beneath my touch, I would have feared not the pitfalls of the Peachtree. I whumped the mouse's ear again and another credit magically appeared. Then another and another and…

"Desist!" roared the AI of Champion. "You must debit as you credit. Haughty cred-its unbalanced by a modesty of debits will earn you the Red Star of Audit from the Royal Tax Collector"

Well, albeit humbled, I'd learned that accounting is amenable, supple and legally manageable if by the gentle stroke of a cursor. By midday, the murk had melted and I was grandly commanding the sacred journey to fill my chalice, rub my back and generally stroke my profit motive.

Meanwhile, our Knight of Production, Sir Andrew of the clan of Walter, folded his arms and beamed an "I told you so, O bewiskered Father." And the fair maid Carolyn swooned, for once again her Knave had been saved from the realm of reluctant poverty.

Great Slobbering Serpents! Did he say starboard was right? Or was it left? Forsooth, I have learned naught!

-30-

Any student who might have passed my accounting course would probably have been a danger to others with the knowledge I would have dispensed, and probably better suited to a career in politics. I never did fathom why *crediting* and *debiting* are more meaningful than *mine* and *theirs*. I'll leave it to the reader to decide whether I might have ruined my students' accounting vocation had I ever exposed my own deficit upon them by becoming a high school business teacher.

When I later launched my first newspaper, I learned that miracles have to come through Proper Channels. We humans don't create them; we don't know the magic words. But we sometimes we badly overinflate faith in our singular abilities. We most certainly are God's helpers in making a miracle work but if it wasn't for that Grand Fellow, we would be like trying to drain the Pacific Ocean with a teaspoon until our genes wore out.

God alone runs the miracle business; he just uses us because we need the experience. Sadly, we haven't learned that lesson and sometimes try to do it ourselves. Then we have to wonder what went wrong.

I did learn, though, that I needed the help of a good money counter. And that turned out to be another little miracle. My son, Andy, had been hanging around the office since college. He was job hunting but hadn't found anything he liked that was interesting, easy and paid a lot. We were discussing our need for a bookkeeper and Andy pointed out that bookkeeping and accounting were pretty simple, at least when he took them in college. Then he showed me on the computer how easy it was for someone with troubled balancing skill. He took over the books and is still professionally satisfying, by all accounts.

By doing our books, he saved us the cost of an accountant—and maybe the newspapers.

Chapter 15

A real miracle occurred the day I met Carolyn Dauel in 1961, I think late August because she was leaving for school the very next day. I was passing through the old hometown on my way to nowhere when I saw an old school chum. We decided to go to Workman's Drive In for a cuppa. Carolyn was there.

Some might think meeting a forever mate as not that unusual. They just met, got married, had kids and worked until they retired. Lots of people experience that. Well, maybe, but since that lucky day I've done an informal polling of many of my friends. Yes, there are some who believe the circumstances surrounding their meeting of their lifelong mates were miracles. And some do not. But I've learned more often than not, those who believed their chance meeting was a miracle also are still in love at middle age and on into the Golden Years. Others, sadly, who believe their "mating" was coincidental don't seem to be as happy. Miracle? I'll take it.

I could call this providential chapter in my life as being at the right place at the right time. If so, I have no doubt God set the ETA. My friend and I had gone to his home to work on a car and decided to take a break. We were heading for the nearest tavern for a beer when both of us, seemingly at the same time, decided to have coffee. We reversed our course and drove to the outskirts of town to a place called Workman's Drive In.

Carolyn and her friend had been attending a church function and before they went home, decided to...yep, have a cup of coffee at Workman's. They were just paying their bill when we walked in. I was smitten and asked for a date. Luckily, she must have been exceedingly bored. She said yes.

The next day, Carolyn left for Colorado Springs to attend nursing school. Before she left, though, she had written the address of the school on a napkin. Not one to put off bliss, I immediately wrote her a note that I would be in Colorado Springs the very next weekend. Fancy that.

My note came back with that very **black** ink the post office loves, "**No Such Address!**"

Looking at that post office heartless stamp, I was a wee bit crestfallen. I'd been given a brush off. Actually, I was miserable, forlorn, and my ego suffered an at least twenty-pound loss of hot air. Months later I learned, to my ego's everlasting relief, she'd transposed a couple street numbers

After a pretty drab period I saw her again, attending a Lenten service at the Loveland Zion Lutheran Church. It just happened the old school chum had called me and asked if I wanted to attend the service with him. Shoot, I didn't know what a Lenten was, but I had never tried one so why not? And there, three pews in front of us was Carolyn. I swallowed what little pride she'd left me and worked up the nerve to ask again for a date—but my chum beat me to it. I was peeved. He was a pretty good friend but I really never forgave him that little exploit.

Things went on for a week or so—I think Carolyn was on Spring break—and I finally got that movie date with her the next weekend. From there, things progressed to a fifty-year romantic cruise.

One of the most marvelous, and I think miraculous things in this world is meeting an angel. Sure, and I know we're Greek-logical (why?) and we end up kidding ourselves: Of course there aren't any angels here on earth. Right?

Wrong. Here comes that detection thing again.

Although they are difficult to recognize, angels are here, all around us just waiting to receive our other-worldly 911 call. The fortunate of us that perceive the experience are changed forever. Sometimes we meet angels in passing and we have a hunch that maybe we've had an encounter but we've dismissed the "inkling" by lunch time. Most times, though, our mind refuses to admit we truly had an encounter with another existence. We may have a transitory thought that a person is special but the real tangible world soon overcomes our flight of fancy and, sadly, we sink back to normal.

Or sometimes, not often, but sometimes, God gives us an insight we never knew we had and, sure enough, by golly, we know… "That was an angel I just met." The *acceptance* of such a notion is the problem here.

Chapter 16

I can't tell you how much womanhood has to do with miracles. No one can. It's just one of those things that is there. I don't know exactly when I realized the truth about Carolyn but I had another experience that got my attention. Before we were married, one night I had this uncharacteristic but strong feeling just before going to sleep. In an unusual moment of unselfishness, I asked God to prevent me from marrying Carolyn if I would not be good for her. Curious, because I hadn't been a church-goer. I'd attended the Baptist Church up to about age twelve when reverence for anything other than my own contentment just started slipping away. From that age until I met Carolyn, belief in anything but me wasn't a high priority.

From that moment on, there was a hunch deep in my mind something weird had taken place. Years later when remembering that altruistic few minutes, my sensitivities for other people reached some sort of fruition. I actually could feel pity for any young man who enters the romantic adventure with his eyes on the young lady's beauty while ignoring the implications of the cost of the marriage excursion. I was so moved at a friend's later wedding, I wrote an advice column about the understanding he would need the very day the honeymoon was over. I've prayed often that if my advice saved one marriage...well, you know.

> *Advice to the lovelorn male*
>
> *There are many things I like about married life. For one, a good wife will always let you know you're unzipped before you leave the house. 'Course there's lots more but it's those little things that a man appreciates when he's trying to impress the boss or asking the loan officer to believe he is responsible.*
>
> *The basic behavior you must learn to enjoy is buying her gifts, except... Do you know how many things can go wrong when a man is turned loose in a shopping center with a credit card and*

has forgotten all those hints she's given him over the past three months and now his only guideline is, if you don't know for sure, spend a lot and maybe she won't get really ticked off when you come home with a dress you are sure will be melt her heart and then you learn it doesn't match her eyes?

To men, blue is blue. To women, it has a touch of grey or it will turn green under certain lighting conditions. But the ultimate sin, it is three sizes too large and the lesson learned is that even an accidental suggestion of obesity is detrimental to conjugal harmony. This is a situation that is not covered in prenuptial agreements and the marriage vows will become meaningless for an unfortunately long time.

This is a basic problem overlooked in the throes of a young man's passion. When a man decides to marry, his mind does not process ramifications in an orderly manner. Oh, he may contemplate how he'll pay the rent or temporarily endure unpalatable meals. He may have considered the cost of the ring as negligible. But somewhere in his male conscious thought will not *be the consideration of how many occasions will elicit the need to purchase a gift.*

No prospective groom considers birthdays, Valentine's Day, Christmas, Mothers' Day (which even if she isn't yet, a gift must be appropriate or the rollout couch is on his "unhappy" agenda). This list doesn't even include all those "little" incidental gifts such as anniversaries, coming home late or forgetting you promised dinner out.

And for each not remembered occasion inciting unexplained silence if you don't get out the door this minute to buy amends, no matter how self-assured you might be, you will experience a complete loss of stability. Of course, nothing you now find will suffice. So many days of a happy marriage aren't because no man really knows what his wife wants. And no matter how many millions of gifts are presented in fancy stores, nothing will find her approval for several days— even a used BMW.

Flowers, candy, jewelry, a fake beaver coat (real beavers have won virgin forest condos from the PETA folks. They spend their time watching their little TVs provided by a beneficent government), can buy you a temporary permit to bliss… but only 'til next time.

I've been married fifty years and the game has not changed. After five decades, what do you get for your wife, for punitive or loving reasons, remains the question. She has everything: You've become a man she's molded to her liking, she possesses her own SUV, enjoyed romantic cruises, has a bulging closet with never the right thing to wear. Doodads clutter her personal home space, purchased over the years by a desperate gift hunter hunting for the forgiveness of foggy planning.

Further, over the years stores have proliferated with a selection of gifts of every description, useless or duplicative; shelves and shelves of kitchen appliances and row after row of unmentionables (which if you do buy, you will soon learn that the gift was for you, not her).

So, young lovers, before you mate, get chummy with a fortune teller who can project during the next several decades just what will be desirable for all occasions. For an extra couple bucks she may consent to warn you about the ever-pending changes brought on by a further mystery called menopause.

-30-

I regret not taking my own advice after writing that column.

But despite my resistance, Carolyn most incredibly changed my life. I actually began

115

to think more often about the feelings of others. I really meant it that cold winter night when I asked God to prevent me from experiencing unearned happiness and I believe that is the first time in my life I really considered someone else before the self-important me. For God's mysterious reason, when I said that prayer, I had become wide awake and wondering what had happened. I can tell you now, it was foreign—and a bit scary to me and it stuck in my craw. I really didn't want to give Carolyn up and the realization that I was willing to do just that frightened the hell out of me.

That was the second small miracle of my life, although I didn't recognize it as such at the time. As the years wandered by, however, it became more and more evident that not only was I an extremely fortunate fellow; something bigger than me was awakened in my mind.

Over the past half century my hunch has grown that I had latched onto a rare happenstance for a cynical future curmudgeon. Everyone loves her and probably always will. I'm constantly reminded at rare social gatherings I attend alone; it's okay that Hank is here, but "Where is Carolyn?" I'm constantly asked. And since she's not actually at the function, people want to know if she's all right.

Understand, of course, that doesn't bother me a whit. She makes excellent gravy, so I don't, ahem, mind her popularity.

The most extraordinary part of all this is that Carolyn does not know she's an angel.

An additional bonus to this miracle meant she saw something in me that might be worthwhile. Personally, if things had been reversed, I'd have sent me packing. Somewhere down deep, though, she saw a redeeming characteristic that she must have felt was worth salvaging. Since that time in 1963, she has been the Princess of the Walter family empire and I have flourished greatly because of her love and patience. Oh, and of course, her inordinately unreasonable ability in dealing with the male ego.

There have been some times… We once had a fight. As far as I can remember, it's the only serious disagreement we've had in all these years. Anyway, we'd been in our first home for about two years when Carolyn decided the living room needed repainting. I reluctantly agreed to help even though a man just instinctively knows when repainting is not necessary. Men just know these things, don't you know, but women, well, they are entirely untrained in why men inherently relate to the old song, "Mañana is good enough for me."

However, pursuit of a career sometimes conflicts with a tranquil marriage. The boys at the office decided one evening we should go have a couple beers after work. I, a budding executive in nascent stage, wanted to be one of the guys. Got home two hours late. Found Carolyn finishing the hallway with unusually firm strokes.

Here is intended to be validation of the superior female instinct when it comes to handling an immature and recalcitrant husband. When it was time to go to bed, Carolyn slept on the couch. Now, consider this. She not only robbed me of martyrdom by not making me spend the night on the couch grumbling at how she didn't care about my career. The injustice! *I* was the one earning the bread and beans. Then, a wonderful breakfast was waiting for me the next morning. She'd humbled herself before I could even apologize, which left me with absolutely no possibility of vengeful sulking.

That rib God took from Adam to create Eve turned out to be a useful male appendage. Yes, sir! It was God's message to all males that U.S. Marines as well as Hell's Angels shouldn't thump their chests too hard. A rib was where their mommy came from.

In the scheme of husband/wife relationships, I was steamrollered; buried under an avalanche of absolute irresponsibility and there was not a thing I could say in my own defense. Since I refuse to be intimidated by the Women's Lib movement (those who say females are superior to males), she must have had some extraordinarily Superior help in putting me in that position of complete grovelhood.

She had deactivated me; eliminated my justification for pouting and achieved a significant diminution to my male self-esteem. I never stayed out late again without calling with a good reason.

Chapter 17

I am reluctant to say here that we've had a perfect marriage, reason being no one would believe me. And they'd be right. Carolyn has a foible or two, I have to admit—although it is not her fault; she's a woman and women do not think as men do. Shopping comes to mind here. Carolyn loves to shop until I drop. I would speculate that many marriages are unwittingly strained for that very reason.

Men are Class B (for bored) shoppers. They know where the underwear department is; three aisles over from the razors after a short detour by the NFL team jersey display. Then it's outta there.

That variance in habits did not come with the rise of Wal-Mart, as any ad agency consultant would love you to believe. No, it came much earlier, in fact very close to the beginnings of the man/woman misinterpretational period which escaped note in the Bible. The best way to illustrate this is that miracles began before men learned to think. In my other job of creating tranquility for those hapless men, I wrote this column just before Christmas shopping fever in 1998:

We don't need "studies" to explain…

…that once again it's the time of year women glow and men grouse, an interlude suggesting there are undeniable disparities in men and women.

Because it's Shopping Time, *a curious season that causes social behaviorists to drool, anticipating that the difference in male/female shopping habits will once again generate scads of government-subsidized studies. For just few millions of dollars, the experts will tell you women like to shop, men don't. It's only a matter of natural biological divergences diversified over the eons by female wiling.*

Look, a woman can labor exhaustive hours running a backhoe, flying a stealth bomber or overpowering felons, but in a twinkling of "Silver Bells," she will energetically grab her purse and be off to the mall for another eight hours with more zeal than the town gossip spreading a juicy rumor about the preacher. Why is this?

By contrast, a man who's just transferred the laundry from the washer to the dryer finds himself lacking the will or energy to decide whether he should buy two bananas or three at the just-down-the-street supermarket. Why is this?

It's not the genes, man. Simply put, I think it's much more metaphysical, going all the way back to cavemen days when the male was the hunter and the female was the cook, whipping up a goulash out of a tough mastodon. The cave man didn't give a grunt whether the meal was roasted, fried or grilled—just how long 'til supper.

The cave woman, though, had to hump that mastodon into the cave, skin the bugger, haul in firewood by the cord and ended her day finally cleaning the bones for grotto utensils. For the next several weeks she whittled the bones down to primitive needles so she could, after drying the mastodon hide, sew a new hunting ensemble for the male hunter/provider/jock.

Meanwhile, after gorging himself and lounging around until the leftovers were gone, the cave man donned his new fur safari jacket with the club holster on the side, gathered the guys and they all went camping, armed with plenty of "Purple Dinosaur Sweat" cocktails and telling lawyer jokes—which were funny even then, although lawyers hadn't yet invented themselves.

Cave woman stayed behind. Someone had to clean the mastodon grease off the kids.

Now I'm not saying this made women smarter through all those millenniums. What it did, though, was make women realize that scraping smelly hides while the men were off frolicking and having a great time in the woods was not Equal Opportunity Employment.

No, I don't have a study to back this up, but I'm betting some politician's aide does. I'll wager what happened was that evolving women took affirmative action. First thing they did was create the notion that not just any old mastodon would do for stew. Say, no mastodon older than 200 years. So, for domestic tranquility, cave men soon found themselves dragging in carcass after carcass until they got the right size and color.

Plus, while sewing up a new loincloth for her hunter honey, that crafty woman put the stiff fur on the inside, which limited the delight of hunting while trudging all spraddle-legged around prehistoric forests. Any man will tell you, spraddling is not fun!

Consequently, it became less and less enjoyable for the men to go hunting. There was that insecurity of trying to guess how many mastodons they were gonna have to daringly chase down before they got a stewable one. It was beginning to feel a lot like shopping...which is why today men experience a debilitating itchiness when their wife mentions the gift list.

Century by century, males just got increasingly discouraged as they painfully brought in inappropriate carcasses. Sudden insight dawned and it came down to about 1948 when men finally understood searching for just the perfect hankie for Aunt Minnie is worse than trying to win a war.

Today, any man will tell you he'd rather eat raw mastodon entrails than go shopping. And a woman? If he's lucky—or in a coma—she'll just smile and say, "Enjoy your ballgame, dear. I won't be gone long."

Modern men and women may have achieved traces of equitability, but shopping skills are a matter of outwitting natural processes. And that, my friends, is why evolution would be mighty unlikely without miraculous creationism. Man needed God to make a woman and the consequences were, in a manner of speaking, a pleasant surprise to him.

-30-

I hope you'll excuse the previous "I digress" moment. It's just that most of my life has been dedicated to determining why men will never, unfairly or not, equal women. And will feminists be happy when they achieve the desired male subservience. My fear is that when the feminine mystique finally disappears into Unisex, all glory, honor and facile enjoyment of Viva la Difference will be relegated to nothing but sighing for a beloved memory. But, 'luckily,' curiosity lives forever.

The legacy of man vs. woman, even though a losing battle for the most determined of warriors, has been the one constant God gave us to continue existing in the face of love. That "constant" is the male inability to recognize feminine wile.

It may be that life will become a person-to-person platonic relationship in the dullest sense, which makes me a little sad. Carolyn and I, by recognizing our dissimilarities, have remained man and wife, lovers, best friends, spouses and sounding boards for each other. Equally important, we've been equals. And as we age, it gets better and better. Why is that? Because maybe we've experienced a tiny bit of what our Maker intended.

What do you know? I guess I hadn't thought of it before now, but there's another of those miracles.

After we were married while I was still pecking tin for dad, we moved into this half-house, half-trailer in the Municipal Park. I suppose it had belonged to a park caretaker back in the formative days of civilization. But it was cheap, it was cute and it stank. Once again, I'd come up against that Thule Toilet Trauma tribulation. The trailer had a jury rigged toilet that seemed plumbed straight to the municipal sewer plant. It smelled like a 1950s junior high boys' locker room, no matter how many blankets we stuffed around the door to our little bedroom/living room.

Although it didn't spit on you if you absent mindedly voided while breathing, as in the Thule Toilet, it would permeate your spirit most indeedly.

Yes, the rent was cheap, but there was a price. We hesitated to go out unless we'd just done the laundry and we invited no friends to visit unless they promised to bring a housewarming gift of their favorite air spray.

Chapter 18

Miracles, I'm sure, are like a Walt Disney fantasy movie to many folks. The bad days and the bad guys are defeated by the Prince and everybody lives happily ever after. But Disney's or Aesop's "Prince" is a fictional character and in most of our lives deep down we think little about his rescuing us from the world we've built around ourselves. Because our lives are "non-fiction" and sometimes we suffer frustration and disappointment when we anoint ourselves director of our own activities.

That's why the Prince of Peace should be met with *our* arms open.

Okay, we've all heard the rephrased old saw, "Money may not buy happiness but it's better than not having it." Sometimes it is, sometimes it ain't. At any rate, wealth so often leads to emptiness, an appreciation of nothing because we have too much of...something. The only way to find that curious inner confidence and gladness is if we're given an opportunity to see the world the way it is and accept the idiosyncrasies of a wildly variable human nature. That's possible only if you have a Mentor to help widen your ability for love and tolerance.

Those of us fortunate enough to accept from God that providential gift of love will find our hearts growing along with self-reliance to such a degree that we will find we can co-exist with the trials and troubles we so carefully craft for ourselves. Only the Mentor can supply that self-reliance with no strings attached.

One of the toughest things anyone can attempt is putting the secular world into perspective. Often it will feel like a never ending search, one constantly interrupted by Satan's whispers about how foolish you are or his favorite, convincing you that only *other* people more mature or stronger than we are can see the light.

One thing at a time. That's the way to discover a new strength growing within us.

Although I was unaware of the reason for it, this was a time for great stress. Deep in my heart I felt I was actually a pretty worthless guy. I was self-centered, selfish, only thinking of my own desires. My deepest thoughts wouldn't have penetrated a pimple. Add to all this the suffering of a depressing lack of self confidence, should have made it plain I was headed to the life of a no-hoper.

I was making no plans nor was I saving any money. I hated every day because I knew the day would be boring. My spirit was listless and I was rude and surly with some very nice people. I was on my way to being a hermit; it's a wonder I didn't take off for the silliness of the California hippy love-in.

I had only one thing going for me: ambition. The problem was, I didn't know and really didn't care where I was going. Having aspirations under those conditions is like walking in your sleep; you move but you don't go anywhere.

It never crossed my mind to look for God except in desperation; "please give me this or don't let that happen" were my normal prayers. That is, until a friend remarked, "Hell is not knowing there's a Heaven." It still took several years before I gave that serious thought but when I did, it began to make sense. My secular life was a real bust. Except for... It occurred to me there was no reason for my believing I was a loser. Yes, there *had* been times when I lucked out, because I certainly had been fortunate in ways for which I suspected were unnatural. Like being offered a hand up into a world I knew existed but really wasn't within my reach.

We'd been married for about five months when one day a gent walked into Walter Motor Company. He was an insurance claim supervisor for a large insurance company and had come to inspect a wreck. We got to talking and he questioned me about my education and plans for the future. I had to admit I had no plan. Then he asked me if I was interested in a vocation related to auto repair but not as dirty.

As I was wiping away the blood and grease from the hand I'd just bashed with the hammer, I was instantly interested. It turned out that mom knew I was never going to be any good at restoring cars to their rightful appearance. She had seen an ad in a Denver newspaper looking for claims adjusters. I had no idea there were such jobs around because at that point I still hadn't learned to think outside *my* box. And here a potential adventure was being represented to me by a guy in a suit.

As he explained the job—and some benefits foreign to a young tin pecker, I'm already looking for the catch; he assured me it was all true. I was delighted. The closest I'd ever come to a company car and an expense account was the time I watched the movie, "The Gray Flannel Suit" with Gregory Peck. First thing I did when I got to my new assignment in Colorado Springs was place an order for a gray flannel suit. It was only later that I learned there was more to the job than an itchy, ugly, baggy-butt hot suit, but I played along for eight interesting years.

I suppose it wasn't really a miracle that someone was looking for someone who wanted the very job the looker was offering. But over the next few years two miracles that occurred in the claim adjusting business most likely would not have happened if mom hadn't seen that advertisement. The first gave me the opportunity to meet with people of varied backgrounds, dispositions and perspectives. I learned that people are not all the same, boring, yet-to-be-useful humanoids. I was beginning to mature—somewhat.

Just as important, when I went to work for the insurance company, my horizons necessarily had to widen. And one eye-opener almost out of this world was the discovery of politics and politicians. Years later, that revelation gave me tons of column material. (Someone once asked Will Rogers, a great humorist of the 1930s, why he didn't use writers. Rogers replied he didn't need writers; he had Congress.)

In my next life as a newspaper publisher (coming soon on a page near you) I ended up writing an assortment of columns about politics and the humor that made writing fun. You may suspect that I was making fun of politicians and sure and you know I was and I am. I don't apologize. Trying to deal seriously with a career politician is like trying to read a newspaper in a windstorm. A little black humor is all us constituents have left that isn't taxable.

Plainly I would not have had those experiences had I stayed in the dark recesses of the body shop world.

First thing, I was provided a plane ticket to the Regional Office in Lincoln, Nebraska, to orientation exercises. As soon as I alighted, right there was a gentleman to greet me, hand me the keys to my "new" company car and show me the way to a nice motel. I got off to a shaky start; I left the windows rolled down on the car and the next morning when I picked him up at his home, I had to explain why I had newspapers laid over the front seats. Shoot, coming from 16-inches- a-year-precipitation-Colorado, I didn't know it rained every danged night in Lincoln.

I was nervous enough to sweat whether I'd still have a job come quittin' time. Didn't have to worry; over the next eight years I screwed up enough to be fired a hundred times—but they didn't give me a pink slip although I don't think my later resignation was surprising to the personnel department.

I have to say, the company was very nice about those rain-swoggled seats two years later when I had to have the rotting upholstery replaced. It was a 1962 Ford four-door dirty gold sedan, probably the ugliest car I'd never dreamed of, but it was beautifully gratis. My mentor explained that the car was for me to chase around innocent victims of State Farm drivers and such, but I could also use it for reasonable personal use and State Farm would buy the gas, tires and all maintenance. I thought I'd had stepped into nirvana.

My first task at the Nebraska home office was to read the company "Claims Manual," a large black four-inch-thick loose leaf notebook containing words I suspected had been invented by an under-worked government bureaucrat. One was "subrogation." I wracked my brain on that one and finally decided it had something to do with underground cornfield irrigation practiced only in Nebraska. This insurance business, me thinks, is going to be difficult. What has growing corn to do with bent up cars?

At the end of my first day, I asked one of the more intelligent acting "claimers" what the word meant. He looked at me, and then looked around the huge cavern of the claims division. He saw a fella heading our way and said, "Sam, why don't you explain to Hank what 'subrogation' means?" Then he shuffled away. (That happens a lot with cubical workers. They lose their will to function in carefree ways.)

Sam, who looked old enough to have denied a claim from Bonnie and Clyde, stopped for a moment and looked at the word. He thought a moment and then turned to me. "I don't know what it means, but it's a word I'd advise you to learn. They don't put those things in the claims manual unless they're important." Then he, too, walked out of the office. I suspect he probably became a middle management supervisor.

That night I found the Lincoln library and attempted to look it up but I couldn't find it. Was it "subjugation,' or "salubrication," or shallow water? You know, it took me a year to find out what that word meant; it was right after I had completed a claim for one of our insureds and the gentleman ask me, "Will State Farm subrogate for my deductible?" As I was still a cub claim jumper, I assured him if there were enough damaged parts left over from his car, the company would certainly subrogate them. I made sure I looked up "subrogation" the next day.

Chapter 19

After returning from Lincoln, where I did not learn about subrogation, I spent a couple days in the Denver claims office before reporting in at Colorado Springs, my permanent assignment. When I showed up the next Monday morning, ready to fly to the heights of careerism, the Denver supervisor chewed me out because I was a day late. I hadn't shown up last Saturday! I told him it was a long honored custom in the Walter family to never start a job before Monday morning. He bought it and told me to go write a repair estimate on a damaged car parked in the company garage.

I had never written an estimate. Dad always did that at Walter Motor Company. But I grabbed a pencil and an estimate sheet and strutted into the garage area and there found an old Desoto (look it up if you care). Its front left fender was bashed in. I first looked to see if there was any blood or guts—I'm still a little squeamish—and proceeded to write the initial bid by Henry A. Walter, Esq. I must have done a pretty good job because the supervisor just grunted, went back to his coffee and donut and sent me to my permanent digs in Colorado Springs. I've always wondered if the owner of the Desoto kept his State Farm Insurance after that claim was overpaid or underpaid.

Colorado Springs was more fun than Denver (fewer people, fewer claims, and lots of loafing). I'll give you fair warning. The New York Times had and has more than once noted that Colorado Springs is the Capitol of "Crusty Christianity," known for its intolerance and out-of-fashion ways. The paper accused Springs citizens of tossing out a couple mayors and city councils who tried to be tolerant and open minded, but we tossed them out because they were trying to lure more company pagans here. The devil lurks in Colorado Springs. Move here at the risk of losing your sense of sanctity for the Godly life, the Times warned. I've often wondered what the Times would do with a story they'd actually investigated in the Springs.

When Carolyn and I dropped our suitcases in our first apartment (the guest house for one of the city's old mansions), the town had somewhere around 75,000 lucky souls. Today, in 2012, the city and county have ruptured to a half million. I'll never forgive the Chamber of Commerce for telling all those "foreigners" what a wonderful place this is. Of course, if they hadn't, our later thirty-year run with our weekly newspapers probably wouldn't have flourished. I cannot say the Chamber is one of those little miracles, however. Chambers are just a necessary evil for the small businesses. You pay your dues and they spend it on incentives to lure big business to the city while the small businessperson applauds as his or her dollars fly away to corporate headquarters in Lower Patagonia or Jersey City.

The first three or four years were filled with blissful goofing off. Then, as the city expanded, the company started sending middle managers to mangle our laid-back lifestyle. Before the "politics" moved into our secluded outstate office, we were pretty much left alone. If we got our work done, we'd go play pool. After a couple years, I got so I was usually finished by noon unless my supervisor had scheduled a visit. At the snooker table I was called "Colorado Shorts," a back-handed referral to the famous "Minnesota Fats" who for years ruled the pool-hall hustle environment.

About this time (1964) Carolyn disconcealed we were going to have a baby. Well, *she* was, but I could sympathetically help by acquiescing to her every wish, even if it meant a trip to the all night supermarket for a jar of olives. It was also that period when I learned that giving in to the lady's strange requests would haunt me for the rest of my life. We got a cat. We have never been without one since, a pox I've carried within myself bravely all these years.

I had not been exposed to domesticated felines before this. Years later I was still so distraught, I wrote a soul healing column warning others about the ways a cat can make us squirm. I would have felt better if the darned cat could read.

You can't punish a cat
One weekend Carolyn and I traveled back east to a family reunion. It was great fun, a wonderful trip and the car made it both ways.

The trip home was uneventful and we were glad to be back.

We got into the house and things started to unravel. See, we were cat sitting for our son who was home for a few days before leaving to work his summer out in the mountains. He brought the "frat cat."

Now I can take cats (preferably staked out on the Interstate). Dogs are okay but cats are sinister. And this cat was sinfully sinister—she's a teenager. She knows how to do things to you that if you could pay her back would cause indefatigable flatulence in the animal rights people organizations.

And she does it with a smile. I know cat aficionados will disagree with that, but if you look closely after a cat has thrown a hair ball between your feet, you will see a slight smirk in their demeanor—like, "So, clean it up, stupid."

I was tired after a ten and a half hour drive. I finally settled into my favorite chair, pulled off my shoes and relaxed to catch up with the back issues of the local newspaper. Whang! Wrapped around my ankles is a cat, kicking and squirming, allowing no escape, claws ribboning my socks and blood vessels. I wasn't quick enough to punt before she was off again, ascending the living room drapes. She knew I was too tired to climb after her.

Later, relaxing and carelessly closing the other eye, my lazy thoughts were jolted by dishes clattering in the kitchen. She'd fallen off the windowsill and knocked the tin water cup into the sink. I really hate the thought of cat prints (even invisible) on tables, counter-tops—my baloney sandwich, but this cat pays homage to no human custom or decree. By the time I got my ax and made it to the kitchen, she was already across the dining room table, scooting for the living room and her hidey hole behind the couch.

The next morning the dog is disgustingly snuffling her body parts when the cat decides dog tails are edible. Our dog's tail is comatose; if an Abrams tank ran over it she'd just look bored and wag the remains. I could use her tail for a stick at a weenie roast and she'd ask only to share. But a cat with a half nelson hold on her tail makes this dog's pituitary gland palpitate.

Things are out of control now, the cat giggling (yes, they do) the dog woofing and me spreading butter on the local news.

My problem is this: How do you punish a cat? They don't accept ultimatums; they just try to play with the muzzle. If you are ever lucky enough to get a firm grip, they punch tiny red holes in your arm. They have such a quick start, by the time you're aware of the nefarious behavior, they're ten yards ahead and climbing.

If you do get in a lucky swat, they go potty in the houseplants.

You never get the upper hand. Our last cat, who died recently from, I believe, a decomposing attitude, never once begged my pardon. For eighteen years I tried to make that cat sorry but she always ended up giving me the slip and then staring triumphantly at me from some unreachable perch, or worse, behind Carolyn who protected her like she was an object of some value.

I didn't hate the cat; I just wanted to hurt her feelings, maybe make her eat broccoli or tie her to the dog's dish just before filling it with beans and gravy (a delicacy Cricket the dog will kill for.)

That never happened. Our previous cat didn't smile like this new nemesis. No, her eyes told you she was an avant-garde species, the same look you get from your Congressman when you ask if the local airbase should be closed.

You can't starve a cat. They find a way to open the fridge. They can find food where you'd swear you'd just cleaned.

So I'm looking for a way to get back as this self-proclaimed prepotent puss. I don't want to maim or permanently injure; just cause a tiny bit of chagrin, to humiliate her so that she knows there's always the chance my inferior intellect will somehow cause her pain or feline frustration. Short of tying her to the engine block of the car, I'd appreciate any suggestions, preferably one I don't have to explain when my son asks why I fried the cat.

-30-

Let me say right here I don't have anything against cats except their snotty attitude. I don't believe cats think they rule the earth and all human species. No, it happens without any conscious thought on the cat's part. Sure they have sharp teeth and claws with which they do not hesitate to use when they feel ignored. It's just...uh... their lack of qualm for making us bleed. I think

God may be a cat lover. Otherwise, why would He give them such efficient defensive weapons while instilling in them a sense of such superiority that they have no reservations about abusing their masters and mistresses?

I guess I wonder why God had to make cats. But I suppose it's like John Wayne's observation: to paraphrase, "A cat's gonna do what a cat's gonna do."

This is the one place I've come to wonder a bit about God's purpose in granting life. I don't wonder about mosquitoes or squids, even tapeworms. They all have a use in this world—at least I believe they do, since God created them. But cats? There must be some explanation.

Chapter 20

I never quite adjusted to adjusting. As far as the company was concerned, I mostly always paid too much on a claim whilst the repair shop owners felt I was squeezing them. And then there was the joy I expressed when I was rarely able to honestly deny a fraudulent claim. I danced on my desk, which was soon reported to the higher ups by one of the other adjusters hoping to gild his personnel file. I had to attend a humiliating breakfast with the No. #3 Big Boss, something young careerists should avoid. Never give the boss a chance to gloat at your expense. It is always demeaning. It can on occasion be terminal if you're unsuccessful at assuming the correct grovel level, a state of mockery many middle managers just love to create in underlings.

It wasn't pleasant arguing with shop foremen and after a few years I was beginning to get unenthusiastic. I tried to justify my employment while trying to maintain objectivity in the negotiations. There were times after a confrontation my sleep came full of twists and turns. Then a coworker taught me one big lesson that at least made four lives easier—the car owner's, the shop foreman's, my supervisor's and, most of all mine. He advised I tell the garage owner to add a few bucks to the repair bill. Then I would deduct the extra few bucks, send the file to the home office showing a "savings" in company money and everyone could remain apathetic.

It wasn't dishonest. No sir, it was a way to foster free trade and agreeable enterprise and it made the company a bit less niggardly in the eyes of the body shop owners. Lobbyists have long thrived on that same human weakness. And, I felt reassurance in that I no longer had to attempt to make good wine out of sour grapes because eighty percent of the shops were honest anyway.

Supervisors accepted that dollar savings because they could report it in whatever reports they had to push up the ladder. It didn't matter if it was the claimant's dollar or the repair shops'. Just save a buck and your bright future with the company was assured. Did you ever consider how much money an insurance company can save on a bazillion claims a year at one dollar a pop?

A bazillion dollar savings a year usually means that the adjusters are doing a wonderful job and will be rewarded for their efforts. During one year of "excessive losses" we hard-working claim jumpers were cajoled and encouraged to save that dollar and in return, we'd be "amply" awarded. No manager or supervisor would elaborate on the award but we were sure the company would be exceedingly grateful for our keeping the company out of dependency on government dispensability. Maybe an all-expense paid visit to the Denver Zoo? Our actual award: A cheap pen set that sits on my desk to this day to remind me not to plan my retirement on a basis of what rewards might trickle to the bottom feeders. Kinda took the steel out of our leaden pencils.

It was soon after that little subterfuge by the Farm that I left the big insurance company. In the eight years I labored there, the seemingly plethora of new managers' changes just seemed to take all the fun out of spending money that wasn't mine.

Part of the skill in being unemployed is to create something. I created sawdust in my home workshop to, I guess, avoid thinking about how impetuous I might have been to quit a good job to search for an unknown one. I wasn't very good at woodworking but I was enjoying just pleasing myself, a natural state for me. That, by the way, is why entrepreneurs keep on trying. Just a bit of columnary advice here before you try to become a home handyman and save money you aren't earning while hypothetically looking for usefulness as a productive citizen. Even unemployed dummies should stay busy just to cause Satan displeasure.

> *Read 'em and weep*
>
> *More and more these days, Christmas gifts come with a caveat: Don't ask for complicated gadgets that require an engineering degree to assemble and use. Otherwise, for days you're saddled with: "Please read these instructions carefully," often suggesting you to have an EMT nearby if you're stupid enough to use the implement prior to becoming aware of its potential lethality.*
>
> *Way too many gifts are, uh, tortuous. Used to be you ripped off the wrapping and enjoyed the rest of the day, waiting for the kids/grandkids to go home so you could run downstairs and use your new anti-splintering salve to repair that board*

you accidently cut with the wrong saw blade (because you hadn't read the instructions).

In today's complex and digitalized world, little can be done without painstakingly studying the guidelines so you won't rashly toss the cat into the microwave after you've crossly run it through the dishwasher.

This year a new Dremel tool was in my stocking. It's a magical thing, able to slice the legs off your workbench or flip a severed finger through the shop when you idly grab the wrong end while it's whirring at 32,000 rpm. It's simple to use when you're awake—unless you read the warnings in the instruction manual. (If you did, the undemanding project can still be an "Indiana Jones" adventure if the sight of your own blood bothers you.) With this little tool that can be slipped into a vest pocket came a thirty-page instruction booklet in three languages, two of which are for countries that don't have electricity.

And, if you do read it before you use it, you will find yourself in such a state of trepidation that a finger might turn up missing before you can find the off button. Because if you believe everything the booklet says can go wrong through impetuous impatience, you'll fear there is absolutely no way to avoid humiliating stares from your neighbors wondering about the flashing ambulance lights in your driveway.

Instruction #1: Do not plug in this tool while swimming laps. It is difficult to call 911 while floating face down. (I am not exaggerating here. I once read a warning label that urged me not to stand on the top step of a ladder because there was a danger of falling.)

This dilemma of fear of fools' tools would be eliminated if the manufacturers of the complexified products ever come to realize the average recipient wants to, without more ado, use his gift tool, not read about it for days before he can drill a hole into an electrical cable hidden in the wall. Or exasperatingly put the offending tool away until the next garage sale. Americans are impatient consumers. Do you know anyone who leaves their new car in the garage for three weeks while trying to fathom the owner's manual which cautions them not to put their head under the hood while driving?

It explains why so many Americans are on depression meds. It ain't the political campaign promises dampening the spirit as much as it is playing with your toys while admonishing yourself with second thoughts: "Maybe I should read the instructions before lighting the Bunsen burner to warm the paint can."

Alright, I know there are folks out there who are gonna rambunctiously rebuke me for cavalierly ignoring an opportunity to enjoy a safe and profitable next February. On t'other hand, when's the last time reading the instructions on your tax forms kept you safe or happy?

-30-

I've a couple times been unemployed, both times on my own culpability because I didn't coordinate my heart with my spirit and didn't know enough to at least *ask* the Holy Spirit for guidance. Yes, it can be fun not having a job if you learn to avoid thinking about it but instead put your intellectual apprehension into something trivial. Like painting the trim on the house with a too-short ladder. Or buying by the numbers from the Super Stores where no matter how much the box says "No Tools Required," you find that even Albert Einstein would have wept trying to solve the vagaries of Japanese or Chinese instructions without a team of engineers needed to install a brick doorstop.

For a year, I tootled around, first as a very part time Body Shop Foreman, Esq. (still writing damage estimates, but everyone has to have a title these days). Six months later I went to work for one of my former insurance coworkers constructing pickup toppers. I left there after he whacked my left middle finger flat with a 10-pound sledgehammer. I have a high pain threshold so I wasn't incapacitated by my lack of health insurance. When the fingernail turned black later that night it was evident some surgery was required if I wasn't willing to let the blood fill it and blow my fingernail away.

I got the tiniest drill bit from my workshop and very *very* carefully hand-drilled into that fingernail.

You must be extremely wary when you determine to heal thyself. Most of the time it's less painful than paying the doctor bill, but once in awhile there is some actuarial risk (I still love those insurance industry terms. They help me pretend I wasn't stupid in bulk in my wasteful years.) I carefully and slowly spun the drill bit with my uninjured hand. I twisted, watching very, very closely for a blood blob to seep through the fingernail, gently relieving the pressure. I misjudged. For those who haven't bothered to talk with an activist lately, nerves are extremely sensitive. They can explode when surprised by a foreign body, such as a cold indifferent steel bit, touches those nerves, most especially beneath your fingernails. I did and I flew seven feet straight up, stopping only because the ceiling was there first.

Thankfully, I learned that self-first aid doesn't render one incapable of pursuing a normal life. Nope. In about ten seconds the pain was gone and I was cured. Of course, Carolyn was upset somewhat when I bled all over her green carpet. We worked it out, though. Well, I did.

I wasn't all that confident the boss hadn't meant to smash my finger. We'd not been getting along well because he was the kind of small business-man that believed coffee breaks were invented by unpatriotic union organizers. I began to have some doubts about my tenure as long as he was nimble enough to swing that danged hammer. He was, after all, getting crotchety.

We had been co-workers at the insurance company but when he got to be boss of the topper empire, he was a trial to work for since I was used to two or three hour coffee breaks at State Farm. You don't do that when you're running your own business and the paychecks depend on whether you work diligently or your brother-in-law is a venture capitalist. I didn't stay around long enough to find out. He was a fairly tough guy and mean as a famished wolverine when he got wound up. Besides, I hated building pickup toppers. There was no challenge. If you've built one topper, they become just like No. 2 pencils: all look alike.

Chapter 21

And so I again walked away from the chance to become a participant in what might someday have become the Apple of pickup topper fame and fortune. A few days later, I was having a cuppa with my friend Don and he came through for me again. He suggested I start my own auto appraisal business. I asked how the heck would I do that?

Well, he asked, did I have a phone, I said yes, doesn't everybody? Do you have an adding machine? I can get one. Do you know where to go to have business cards printed? I can find out. And that, ladies and gentlemen, is how Hank the Crank went into business for himself. Funny how a vocation serving a big company gets to be mundane, monotonous and finally miserable but doing it for yourself can be marvelous, magnificent and merry. Still, entrepreneurship could be defined as going on a blind date. You never know what you're getting into until it's too late to have a headache.

One big mistake for me was not facing up to another known curse Satan uses so very well was the fact that I would never be good at coping with unhappiness and anger every day, so I left the whimsy of a good paycheck, a company car, an expense account that was pretty good, and health insurance. For some reason, I had neglected to ponder the prevailing consensus that the average American cannot exist without health insurance. Later the government revealed the danger I faced and decreed me to be insured in order to be whole, but that was years later, too late for me to retreat from my venture into free enterprise.

My ignorance of the dangers softened the risks of earning an entrepreneurial living without support from a big company, the government or an imprudent rich uncle. It was another of those little miracles I so often recall these days. I was just too self-absorbed to worry about the odds against me. I had read somewhere that of all the small businesses started every year, the probability is about forty-nine out of fifty will fail. Had I known that, I probably would have remained a drone until someone told me I had a vested interest in Social Security and I could retire to futilely cope with five "extra Saturdays" sans expense account or petty cash—you know, that few bucks you always had in pocket which now goes for things like wet wipes.

I should have been afraid and would have had I known then how naïve I actually was. Me, a businessman? Yahbut… Y'know, working for someone else means you have one, or maybe if you're not indolent, two jobs necessary to keep the bacon coming. Starting, out, you don't want to think about the IRS, the FICA, the supply expenses or that when you work overtime, there's no extra in the pay envelope. There's often no pay envelope.

My best skill was dreaming and that doesn't even pay minimum wage. Business folks, I'd always surmised, were of a higher breed than I, possessing all these smarts and talents—and—grit…perseverance, those characteristics not always available to the bourgeois with dirty hands. The only thing I had going for me was remembering what I'd learned after I'd taken that high school IQ test. I could qualify as a wool gatherer. (Not a sheep shearer, a *thinker*!) I was a dreamer with ambitions unbeknownst to me, which is as good a definition as any. But, and this is a big but, for those who think they can't succeed as an entrepreneur, they have to rationalize. I examined what that counselor had said and it came to me: a good entrepreneur is one who doesn't take risks seriously. Or regular eating habits, for that matter.

Another miracle? I'm not sure, but it did prove that anybody can do anything, even become President of the United States if he or she doesn't fear the media and doesn't study the pitfalls of self reliance—like unfixed working hours, regular meals…like that. (Although…if you don't have any reason to fear the media, you're probably too boring to become President.)

Of course, my having a goodly bit of naiveté about the commercial world didn't hurt. And I had some help. Carolyn, after some cajoling, "volunteered" to be my secretary and appointment taker. I had a sort of office in our basement and from there it was a matter of making sure the ends would someday meet the needs. First thing was to call every insurance adjuster I'd ever dealt fairly with on a mutual claim; then go to his company and ask for the overflow claims; and lastly, buy a parts and labor manual that everyone used in those days. Oh, and a hand-cranked adding machine of dubious age and accuracy. Lesson: don't buy new if you know a good junk man.

Here's another lesson for those who want to be a businessman. "Starting from scratch may be difficult but starting without it is really dumb." (Dr. Laurence Peter)

I had little grasp of what I was doing, but of one thing I was certain; if you don't ask for business, you don't get business. Within about three months, I had several insurance companies calling me (or Carolyn) and it wasn't long before the checks started rolling in. Of course, the "rolling checks" were like a lazy dog: they rolled only when the sun moves.

We made it through the first six months by judiciously starving. As I have said earlier, I was only an average adjuster, but with some refinement in manners, I could probably write an estimate and sell it to the garages I hadn't already offended in my other life as State Farm Insurance Employee #1008988007½. I had a teeny speck of equivocation when I had to visit a couple of those repair shops I'd been so stingy with company money. But I swallowed hard and donned my newly acquired demeanor, worked up a smile and walked in like I was a professional worthy of respect.

Thing here, you must understand, is those repair shop owners needed business just like anyone else and so most—not all—took my estimates and profited by it. Obviously, I was writing the estimates that included a bit more prime rib than I had with the "Farm." Being an independent, though, I needed the shop owners' good will as much as I needed the insurance companies'. If I couldn't sell the job on a reasonable basis, the insurance companies would sure as heck find someone who could. I mellowed in a hurry.

Inexplicably, I became Gentleman Henry, the Professional, Friendly, Compromising, Dealing and Wheeling Walter Appraisal Company. It was a successful enterprise for awhile—until I got ambitious and took in a couple partners. My thinking was the more estimates we write, the more money we make. Things didn't work out.

It probably was a combination of lack of knowledge, incomprehension and the realization that I was not qualified mentally or emotionally to attain the results gained by my newly acquired chutzpa, but we made a little money. Despite my limited knowledge of business practices or experience, we survived. The only thing I knew about a "business plan" was they have to be changed more often than day-old quadruplets.

Someone was watching over me and I actually began to learn from my mistakes, a new and almost implausible habit for me.

We grew and prospered, despite our limitations and lamentations. Why? As I've said, I began to comprehend there was more to life than just good luck. I had long believed in prayer, mostly for a winning lottery ticket or a BMW sport car someone had carelessly misplaced. As the appraisal business continued to flourish, I began to ponder a bit more cognitively about what I might have done to trigger all the breaks I was receiving. Nothing came to mind. I can tell you, though, it made me progressively more humble.

The appraisal service grew to sixty-four client insurance companies. The work rolled in. Problem was, my two lieutenants didn't seem as much in a hurry to get rich as I did. Along about this time, I also began to reckon that writing repair bids for damaged cars was about as stimulating as buying underwear—unless it was for Carolyn.

As I ruminated my repetitive, exciting-as-hoeing-corn life, a mini-revelation began to grow in my thus far day-to-day regularity. I recalled the time a history teacher had asked why I was day dreaming despite a test coming up. Thinking quickly, I yarned into a long explanation that in my previous life, I was a swamper in a 1900s New York City Bowery saloon. It was a good job, I assured her, because I could live on the day-old peanuts, dill pickles and the boiled eggs the bartender let me have as part of my salary. Sort of like tips today. My "story" seemed a good joke at the time and I'm sure it aided my postponing maturity.

I'm fairly sure I flunked the exam. Too many teachers are remiss in recognizing the remarkable power of meditation. How else is one to find the time to recognize miracles?

Thinking back on that moment even today, I get nostalgic. I might have run into The Great Gatsby" and his romantic gang in my earlier saloon life. And since I had free use of the barroom piano after I'd cleaned the spittoons, I figured someday I might have been discovered and become another half of a Rogers and Hammerstein incredibly successful duo thrilling Broadway crowds. Ah, the magic of Broadway musical composers/lyricists. It's depressing to consider the creative talent in this world that goes to the grave unrequited because of limited dream power.

I was not a sagacious dreamer; more an optimistic romanticist. That's probably why I remember high school as a playground. I never really let go of recess. The rest of it? Aahh, it was okay, but I wasn't planning to make my living at something like dissecting a frog. My real life ahead just hadn't crossed my mind as of yet.

Curiously that advice from an English teacher meant less than that of a jock. Halfway through my junior year, I had decided to drop out of school and go make my fortune. A couple friends were plotting to go to Oregon and work for one's uncle in a—get this—a fish processing plant. Wow! Fish gutting for a living. On our own. No tests or finals. Our own spending money; certainly more than we'd ever seen. Change underwear only when we wanted to.

Going all the way to Oregon sounded like a great adventure for a young man of seventeen with a limited vision of poverty. But it didn't happen. At the time I was wrestling at 103 lbs. I was pretty good. Not great enough to win any tournaments, but I won most of my matches, so I had some adolescent notoriety around school. Word got around about our fish scraping plans and one afternoon, the coach took me aside before practice and asked me if I thought I was smart enough to learn a couple new moves on the mat. Sure, said I.

Coach stared at me for a moment and then shook his head. "Nah, I don't think you are." I was astonished. He walked away and I knew, as the kids say today, I'd been "dissed." Whoa, he couldn't do that to the inimitable Hank Walter. I ran after him and asked him what he meant.

"Well, if you're dumb enough to want to quit school, you're too stupid to learn anything that I might teach you."

I went to practice that afternoon a puzzled pup. I liked the coach and I thought he liked me. But his appraisal of me was like a punch in the gut. During that practice, I determined to prove to that pompous sounding coach he was wrong. I stayed in school, graduated and then several years later I realized it was a wonderful break that a crusty, cauliflower-eared ol' coach changed my life. It was the one time I seriously considered my future and I didn't know who to thank. Before, I hadn't respected the coach's opinion that much. Odd how life works; had I quit as a junior I probably would never have learned to write *and* chew gum.

As I grew older and learned not to be so obtuse, I began recalling other "good breaks," things that

I had done reflexively or, more often, not done, like getting into the Marines and probably maiming myself trying to succeed in a career at which I could never have excelled. I did so many things wrong that later turned out right. Know what I mean? Sure you do. Think about it.

Chapter 22

I've never considered myself particularly lucky. Well, sure, I've won a few door prizes through the years, like maybe a free dinner at the local Annie's Hotcakes and Sauerkraut Diner. Never won a lottery, though. And the day I won the baseball pool at the office was the day Carolyn won five times as much on the pool where she worked. I threw away my rabbit's foot.

Where do miracles come from? And why, all of a sudden was I searching for them? How on God's Green Earth could I suspect I might be blessed? I'd done little to save the starving masses in Third World countries. I had spent no time serving in a soup kitchen in our town. The little I put in the offering plate at church wouldn't have bought a free meal for a hobo.

I finally began to realize there is only one possible source for miracles, those co-incidents turning ambiguous intentions into good fortune. I think it was when I began to give thanks instead of just wondering why God answered my haphazard "Help Wanted" prayers. Just when I got to figuring there might be some secret code needed for this prayer thing, little things just seemed to go my way. Later on in life I finally began to awaken and reflect that some pretty big things had occurred on my way to becoming a Centrum Silver vitamin addict.

It was a revelation, coming to appreciate what I had and have. It's funny how starting to say thank you seemed to minimize the fears of and for this confounded world. So, maybe, just probably another "miracle" gave me hope and some kind of insight. I still don't understand but I'm not going to question it.

It's a possibility that decision to stay in school and learn how prepositions could relate to other words or whether to gut fish influenced me to, after another eight years of independently trying to make people happy with the results of mistakes drivers made, I decided I was frustrating my destiny counting hail dents and then having to roll the dice with the garage foremen ala "Let's Make a Deal." I decided to take a year off from the world. I was re-experiencing an undaunted audacity that I previously had ignored in my perusals.

Just asking for fulfillment won't do it. I had to learn to pray within my own humility. Doing it "My Way," as Frank Sinatra used to sing, can give you trouble, such as a long term in perdition. Independent thinkers must indeed possess great persistence within their quest for success and/or tranquility. Otherwise you could end up wasting your whole life wandering in the mud of self doubt.

Now here is a pretty good time to advise anyone who is contemplating striking out on their own instead of occupying a cubicle in a large, air conditioned building that frowns at you every morning at 8:30. I sold the appraisal business; I walked away as if a great weight had been lifted from my id, ego and super ego.

I was partially emerging from the trap I'd laid for myself, that of caring first for me. But I soon learned that events don't always work out as expected.

The sale of the company was an honest transaction and the buyer knew exactly what he was getting into. However, about four months after the sale, I received a notice that I was being sued by the buyer. I was shocked and all I could think of was calling the lawyer for the two still involved lieutenants to learn why I had been branded as a civic scoundrel.

Never got a clear answer (or if I did, it was so petty, I've forgotten it). What I did, though, was pay three monthly bills for about four or five hundred bucks. Like a fool, I paid it out of my dwindling savings. Finally one day I called the remaining "lieutenant" at the appraisal service, also a "defendant" in the lawsuit, and asked what his lawyer was telling him.

"Not much?" he answered. I suggested we meet for lunch. I told him I wasn't paying another nickel and he could do with the lawyers what he wanted. If they wanted to sue me, that was their foolish prerogative. I was broke anyway. (I lied a little but not much.)

A funny thing happened on the way to justice. The two lawyers seemed to rapidly realize us illiterate peons were about to rebel and there was no further profit to be apprehended. The lawsuit disappeared—along with a chunk of my petite nest egg.

The lesson here is that most lawyers are honest; some are qualified, some are civic minded and humane—and some few took the "hypocritical oath"—just like in any other profession. It was the first time I'd come up against the legal system where I was, of all things, a target of a litigant calling me a thief. I spent a good chunk of money before I realized I had to staunch the bleeding—which to this day I believe was only a scheme set up to collect a fee. I don't know that, but during the intervening years, I've learned not everyone is a saint. It is a great lesson for would-be entrepreneurs: When there is no full explanation offered, there may be no validation. If that's the "case" against you, stand up and say STOP!

Just a couple years after my escapade with lawyers and had entered my paramount newspaper business adventure, my uncle D.T. Lawson came to visit. He had some interesting takes on small business people and lawyers in our town. His most interesting insight hit me as being spot on for an entrepreneur trying to keep an eye on using his or her head in striving toward success before hoping high tech will guarantee it. Computers are fine but they don't sweat. And sweat equity is a critical ingredient in attaining any goal.

Haystack therapy

My ol' uncle Dubious T. (Call me D.T.) Lawson visited last week. D.T. was born and raised in Half Dollar, Texas, (formerly Two Bit before farm subsidies). Half is an old fashioned town; genial folks, hardworking and ready with advice. Nosy.

D.T. was impressed with the friendly people in our town. "Comin' up I-25, I's tickled how many folks waved as they passed me," he opined. Waved, I asked? "Yup, a real Half Dollar salute."

A Half Dollar salute is a casual forefinger raised an inch off the steering wheel, so I didn't ask if he'd noticed which finger was being waved as he poked along the interstate at 55 mph on our 75- to whatever mph you think will slip by the State Patrol radar.

"Yessir," he went on, "a young feller pulled alongside and yelled, 'Hey, gramps, whyn't you get out'n walk?' By golly, Doc Grimsley made that same point two weeks ago!"

I really admire D.T. He's that good sort who suspects our tarnished side just needs a bit of polish now and then. "You got some real 'hygeenetic folk 'round here, too," he said. "Saw a young lady scootin' long, just acombin' away at her hair. Wouldn't do that myself; kinda like pickin' your nose in a stampede," he observed. "Handled that little car like a bred cuttin' horse, though."

"Saw a fella shavin' too. Couldn't tell 'it was a safety razor since he seemed purty anxious to be somewhere else. Bet he looked good if he got to where he was aheadin'. Hope he had on clean woolies fer the ambulance driver."

D. T. is a rosy philosopher. He believes politicians are abidable. "They don't steal any more than back in the 30s and 40s. It's jes inflation makes it look so. B'sides, with the retirement they're stashin', most of 'em should soon have enough."

They don't have cable TV in Half Dollar, so when D.T. clicked on MTV, he got a surprise. "By golly," he remarked, "them fellas sure do sound like they got on the wrong end of the knife at gelding time."

Ol' Unc was awed by the large size of our phone book. While perusing, he came upon the fifty-seven pages of attorneys. "Wal, I'll be danged, I don't b'lieve we have that many in JAIL in Texas!" The only crime D.T. recollected was when Duff Pendergarten stole Ivy Malone's goat and ate it.

"Guess we've just never seen the need of no lawyers ner trial. We jes put 'ol Duff to work splicin' Ivy's fences around her sow barn. He got to likin' her cookin' so much, he up and married the widder. Fer the price of one goat, she got the cheapest hired hand in West Texas 'n she lets him sleep in the house now and then. Nobody gets too riled at the judicial process in Half Dollar, long as everyone gets what they got comin', whether they want it or not."

While visiting the newspaper offices, D.T. noticed a guy at the picnic table next door using portable lap top and cell phone. I pointed out that's the way business is done these days. "Mebbe so," D.T observed, "but afore long, that fella is gonna feel the need to flop back on the sunny side of a soft haystack. And I ain't seen a lotta haystacks in Colorado Springs. Mebbe you folks are apushin' your tensile limits."

As he said that, I self consciously put my feet up on my desk.

-30-

Chapter 23

One would think one would learn, by his or her experiences, at least a modicum of don't-do-thats. You don't spit on a hot stove. You don't buy your mistress flowers with your wife's credit card. Don't bet on the Cubs to win a World Series. Above all, don't think you are *not* swift enough to run a business. Just follow the simple rules I've laid out earlier, rules I learned through do-overs, stop- that's and prayers the stock market doesn't hit an angry Bear market six months after you've mortgaged all you own except your tent. You may be just putting off forever a great adventure.

Of course, you must submit yourself to the ages-old psychological test: Do you possess at least one of these three emotions: Courage, cowardice or angst? That was the question asked of me when I showed my plan to another friend who had his own business. He said with no uncertainty the first conclusion I must reach is whether I'm brave, a fool or acting out of desperation to avoid work.

During a prior one-year escape from rationality, I had begun writing a novel, a wonderful example of starting a project with a limited chance of success after selling the appraisal business; you don't try to write a book with the hope you will be published and make money just before your nest egg runs out. The only way your book will achieve eternal perusal is if you are a politician or by becoming a Hollywood celebrity. It may take the rest of your productive life to get a publisher to buy enough paper to put out a first book. That is not good. In fact, it may terminally delay your book signing.

Nine months later and leaner, I began to suspect I wasn't going to sell the book. What that meant was, if I don't shave, take a bath and look for a job, I soon might have to sell our house. Selling wasn't feasible because my equity at the time would amount to moving into an old chicken house abandoned somewhere out on the dry and lonesome eastern Colorado prairie. If you think about it, that is not a recommended way to retain creativity. There are few outlets there on the plains; I don't know where I would have plugged in my typewriter.

I had another problem, too. I was 45 years old, had gained barely a bit of what was surely questionable business experience, and was extremely reluctant to sell myself for what I suspected I was worth to an employer. About the time Carolyn was ready to force me into productive animation, a friend asked me if I'd be interested in writing for a local weekly newspaper. I applied and got the job.

I loved it. Going around talking to the police about some uppity who got arrested last night. Or the local city council fighting about whose fault it was the waste disposal plant overflowed. Sometimes the stories were interesting, like those about local folks who did something dumb, brilliant, abnormal or sued their neighbor because his cows were spewing methane. I was really a cub reporter in the truest sense.

Just as I was beginning to think this newspaper reporting might be interesting the owner decided he was paying me too much and fired me. He wasn't gentle about it. One night five months after I became a cub and just before I could legally hit him for unemployment benefits (and after we'd put the paper to bed for that week) he called me into his office and poured me a drink. Was rotgut and I didn't cipher the awful taste it was going to leave in my mouth. As we sipped away like ol' buddies, he said, "You're fired." Huh? "I can't afford you. I can get any monkey to write news stories and if I don't keep 'em around long, they don't get uppity and begin to think they're journalists."

I was stunned. It was like that Billy goat of my youth had finally caught up with me. "Oh, by the way," he said, "I'd like you to come in tomorrow and help me deliver the papers to the carriers." I thought about that for a moment and then asked, "Do I get severance pay?" That was the first time I'd heard him laugh, sorta like a cow that needed milking.

So there I was on the street, looking for a cup of coffee that I couldn't afford. The sky was darkening and it began to rain. Just as I was heading for shelter at the local cafe I ran into a friend who said he'd buy. Well, not a close friend, but a member of our church's congregation. We'd sung together in a quartet a few times, but I really didn't know him well.

A major miracle? One of the biggies, as it turned out. The interlude was a life swapper!

Don was president of the local bank but it had recently sold. Naturally he was let go because no bank owner wants a president who knows more than he does. However, being a terrific bank manager, Don was soon hired to be president of a new neighborhood bank in a very exclusive area of our town.

He'd been at his new position for about six months and he had a problem. Any business that wants to succeed must advertise its services. However, the local daily newspaper was e-x-p-e-n-s-i-v-e! With my now sullied and shortened career at the weekly newspaper in ruins, I guess he suspected I'd be open to an off-handed suggestion that I launch a newspaper in his advertising area.

How we ended up in that particular restaurant on that particular day at that particular time, I've not questioned. My ship hadn't come in but it was approaching the harbor! I almost missed the boat, though. At first I had a good laugh at the mere thought of me, Hank Walter, launching a newspaper. I had no inkling of how much ink I'd need. I didn't know how to sell advertising. I didn't even know how you laid out Page One.

The proper use of a pica pole never entered my mind. As far as I knew, "pica" was the name of some deadbeat ne'er does well.

I mused about the idea for an hour or so and then, without further astute cogitation, I drove out to the bank's neighborhood called "The Broadmoor" (after the hotel of international fame and the prideful centerpiece of the city of Colorado Springs) situated in some of the most beautiful rolling hills of Colorado Springs and reconnoitered; did a "marketing" study, like how much office rent this fancy locality would ask. Not really knowing what to ask or from whom. I drove by the administration building of the local Cheyenne Mountain School District 12 and on impulse, I stopped to see the superintendent of schools.

Also not knowing how the big boys played the game of parlaying a nonentity into a feasible venture, I flat-out asked, "How'd you like a newspaper in your school district that would report all the great things you do here?" Insinuating, of course, that it would be a "friendly" sheet, not one searching for dirt about the school treasurer taking fine vacations in Tibet.

The super was thrilled and took me by the hand to go meet the other bank president in the neighborhood. That president, too, was all for it and promised a good advertising budget would be worked up, aimed my way—if I could get the newspaper off the ground.

Now I had two bankers, and a school superintendent that wasn't afraid to ask any of the local upscale businesses for whatever the schools needed. I continued around the neighborhood talking with other businesses and the day after Thanksgiving, 1982, I had something for which to really be thanking God. Don's bank grubstaked me to the tune of a few thousand dollars and I was off and running. Where, I had no clue and no map and was too naïve to know I knew nothing. But I suspected there was gold in them there hills.

And that's when I finally became aware that miracles do happen. These guys had faith in me, a closet nitwit who had an urge to write—whatever, while I knew I wasn't even capable of causing a cat some chagrin.

I have to say, from that November 1982, I have found more happiness and fulfillment than I'll ever deserve. Things fell my way so often, I soon lost track of good luck, good fortune, smart thinking and, as it happened, very good timing economically in our town.

I must admit, however, that I had some doubts about our financial viability. I soon found myself writing a column about the trials of launching your boat before checking for leaks.

Here's one column delineating my naiveté.

It takes courage to be stupid

Was chatting the other day with a reformed bank examiner as he speculated on why anyone with a licka sense would choose to be a small business owner. Congress is always whittling away at Big Business, making laws that cost the big boys big bucks, laws that the small business person is ill equipped to read, let alone understand and be compliant. Which explains why, by living under the politicians rules, most small business owners have to learn to live on a wage that most people would consider a lousy tip.

Well, now, I pontificated, folks want to be a small business person so's they can have the freedom to do what they want without having to go through obtaining "official" permission to make a paper clip chain. (I thought big in those days.) Small business folks have an abiding desire to blaze their own trails, challenge the odds, and reap the glories of independence from muddling middle managers who make rules re: our behav-ior/etiquette on and off the job. We are entre-preneurs, (I later looked the word up) meaning "Person who values the right to be wrong in his or her Rorschach test."

I think about here I realized that I could be a successful newspaperman; I didn't know what the hell I was writing about but it felt good putting it on paper.

Entrepreneurs may be the last whimpering remnants of the great American pioneer lust. Who else but a small business person, without a battery of corporate attorneys, would want to confront the specter of jousting with the IRS armed only with rules the IRS itself admits it doesn't understand? Who else, armed only with a seldom read New Testament, but a small businessperson would read constantly about the high cost of survival as specified by bureaucrats, guardians of the public trust and still send a check for the latest tax due before calculating your own paycheck?

I can't speak for other small business people but around the Walter Publishing Empire, I took pride in knowing the importance of being in charge. In large businesses and especially in big government, no one is in charge except the financial gurus. There's always a board or department or committee making the final decisions and no one will be held personally responsible for, barring an indictment, while staying just a bit anonymous and can claim ignorance in case the buck stops at his or her cubical.

In a small business those decisions are made by the guy who usually empties the wastebaskets. Like who is going to clean the bathroom today? The President. Who unclogs the stopped-up toilet? The CEO who gets to take the calls from fast talking New York stockbrokers? The Chairman of the Board, that's who, because in a small business, everyone else is playing a critical role. And that makes the small business owner/president indispensable if for no other reason than if these tasks are not taken care of, the really important people –the employees—get a bit testy when the bathroom reeks.

There are other perks. The small businessperson is treated royally by a legion of entities. For instance, the small business owner/slave (newspaper publishers, anyway) will get invitations to swanky functions. Along with that recognition *will be an offer to buy a "corporate table" for $5000 or so, which means you can give your employees the pleasure of attending black tie functions and rubbing shoulders with the President of AT&T. But the business owner can't go. At the moment, his tuxedo is in the unaffordable men's store.*

It's flattering to be considered one of the VIPs in your little town when you get a reputation of making enough money to flip out $50 or $100 or maybe $10,000 to be a patron of this year's rubber duck regatta in the local brook proudly called a "crick" by the local worthies. It's a downer when you've just gotten back from your annual Friday afternoon through Sunday night vacation in downtown Pumpkin Center only to learn the newspaper office has been burgled.

Ah, but that sense of power in being your own boss, you may sigh. Where you and only you can say when you will arrive in the morning and what time you will close: Before dawn, after bedtime.

It's the president/owner/big chief who gets to explain to the employees the economic value of recycling the toilet paper; whether to beg the banker to extend your note or whether or not to ask your spouse to take in laundry "…just until I can get the thing on its feet."

Oh, did I mention the fertilization of your ego as a small business person? The employees always keep the boss foremost on the information front. For instance, do you know who is the first to know the coffee pot is empty? Or that the printer is out of paper and someone had better go get some or there ain't gonna be no work done in this here office, Mr. High and Flighty pooh-blisher!

I recently read about a high level temporary college administrator who will work for only 10 months and make more than a hundred grand. A small business owner may have courage and grit but none I know would have that kind of chutzpa. Of course, had he or she known of the generous pay an educator can command, they might have shucked off that entrepreneurial pride and donned the robes of academia.

But I doubt it.

-30-

Chapter 24

So...there I was, by a mysterious miracle, a newspaper owner. I had a bank loan; I had leased an office; moved in an old roll top desk that had belonged to my dad. I had a wife who was willing to serve as an unpaid slave for, oh, maybe six months...just temporarily until I got on my feet, don't you know.

What didn't I have going for me? I was unaware I was still not ready to compete with the local daily newspaper. I didn't have a sales person. I didn't have a camera. As I fingered my BIC pen, I suspected there was an acceptable way you published a newspaper but I'll be danged if I knew what it was.

I asked myself: If I'm going to have a successful venture here, what is the first thing I should do? Then this brilliant idea hit me. I'll call some other weekly newspaper publishers around the area, pretend I know what I'm doing and get their reaction. Surely, if I listened carefully, I'd learn something about the business. Surely.

First guy I called had three words of advice. "Don't do it." The next three were "You're an idiot." And finally, "Do you even know what the inverted triangle is?" Well of course, said I, but what in the world has that to do with putting out a newspaper? After he hung up, I made a note on my to-do list to call the community college and sign up for a journalism course.

The next publisher listened to my "presentation," and then suggested I buy him out. I hung up. The last was more helpful. "Do you know how to write a news story?" When I admitted I was a little out of practice, he suggested I might want to learn before I published my first issue. He was laughing as he hung up. Well, I thought, that's encouraging. He sure sounds happy to be a newspaperman.

With all that encouragement, I never looked back. Or forward, either. I enrolled in the local community college, certain in my own mind this newspapering had to be a pretty simple process, albeit more challenging than wall papering. I mean, if a guy has to ask me what an inverted triangle is he must be pretty dumb. The way it works, according to my business plan is, you write. People read. You make money because the readers buy from your advertisers because they're so thankful you are telling them all about the neighborhood news.

And then you win a Pulitzer Prize.

It wasn't that I was so optimistic. I just didn't consider pessimism—which may be a reason we have so many small businesses in this country that are successful; thinking only gives you reasons *not* to do something you've never attempted before. You ever stop to think how many things wouldn't get done in this world if people realized all the extra work they're creating for themselves? If we stopped to consider the pitfalls beforehand, the United States would be a nation of politicians and welfare recipients, many of whom would never contemplate working for a living.

Thinking back, I have no doubt that wonderfully clever banker was the messenger with the third greatest miracle of my life, right after claiming my citizenship as soon as they yanked me from my mother's womb and then capturing my very own angel, Carolyn. Why shouldn't I be optimistic about my odds of success? Here it was Wednesday and I was actually thinking ahead. There must be an omen in there someplace.

Again, a reminder. You must learn to remember all the miracles so that you can later set them apart for re-study. Otherwise you could end up as a swamper at the local bar and grill. There's a danger in shrugging off what you dismiss as maybe only an unworkable flight of fancy. So, be upbeat, self assured and whistle a happy tune. Take charge of your destiny! Oh, and also damn the torpedoes.

You could be a unique person and end up with the leprechaun's gold if you had listed the "suspected" miracles at the time they happened! A word of caution here: In the elation of the moment, Satan is ready and willing to take credit for miracles and convince you this or that was simply good luck, especially those small ones which are taken in stride. Learning the source of your lucky breaks is tough but when you ask for divine guidance, for crying out loud stop and listen for an answer! Listen with all your might because God seldom, if ever, shouts.

I've talked here a lot about the miracles in my life, but one thing became clear to me as I roamed on my journey to journalism: Most of us take the credit ourselves because we're afraid to accept something we don't understand or believe we deserve or, at the worst, decide to have lunch instead of contemplating what at first glance seems inconceivable. There's a joke that fits here. Guy is late for an important meeting. He can't find a parking place. "Please, Lord, help me find a parking place," he pleads. He drives around the block a couple times and still no space. "O God, please help me find a parking place." He turns the corner again and there's a space right in front of him. "Oh, never mind. I found one."

We don't recognize miracles. We don't comprehend miracles because we have deemed ourselves to be sophisticated in our modern world. People who believed that stuff about wonderful phenomena and spirits were dumb and besides, they're all dead today. We, you and I, are too clever to kid ourselves that parking place was probably there all along and we just missed seeing it. Just a happy coincidence.(?)

Miracles are sly. Sometimes they can cause pain before jubilation. Take childbirth, for instance. And, too, some miracles take years to mature, leaving you ignorant of the beginning of making you a "what, where, when and why" reporter you've become and ended up in the catbird seat. It's tricky to connect something that happened fifteen years ago with what's good and wonderful today.

The miracle of "miracles" is when you *know* and *believe* deep in your heart one took place. I didn't for one second consider I had experienced a miracle when I sat down in that little one-room newspaper office and asked myself, "Where to now?" But marvels began to occur almost from the first day. First, I had a built-in office manager. Carolyn is extremely (is superiorly a word?) good with people and I've never discerned anyone who has ever met her who doesn't enjoy dealing with her. (I'm not the only one that has described her as an angel over the years.)

She took over the office and the phone calls while I deliberated over my first news story. Later, she took over the classified advertising and her phone manner began to draw in more of the little but invaluable ads, sometimes enough to buy lunch. As I watched her in action, I'd swear some advertisers came back just so they could talk to this fascinating lady.

I didn't think of her as a miracle then (free labor) any more than I realized Eileen Carter was a miracle. I was too busy worrying about making a living off this little "weekly wiper" than I was about everyday progress.

But Eileen occurred. Eileen was a new member of our church congregation. Somehow she heard that Carolyn and I were starting a newspaper and she came to see us about the job of typesetter. I couldn't afford a typesetter. That would have to be my nonpaying job. I asked if she'd ever sold advertising. No, but she was willing to "give it a try," she answered.

Voila, she was on board.

I set up the roll top desk, squeezed it into the corner of that bitty office. She sat down and looked around, then up. That was when she noticed there was a two- by six-inch hole in the corner of the roof. You could see blue sky (a good omen for a new business). We went to work. Not everyone can see the blue skies of Colorado when they work. And Eileen was not one to let a draft spoil her parade.

I prayed it wouldn't rain.

It wasn't a week before she had every nook and cranny of that desk stuffed with business cards, call-back notes, appointments and, yes, real, paying advertising copy. And, to my complete and joyful surprise it wasn't too many years before she became one of the best (if not the best) advertising sales person in Southern Colorado. And, some-what to my disgruntlement, she became one of the best paid advertising sales persons in Southern Colorado. The very first week, I seem to recall, she brought in enough advertising inches to give us the wherewithal to do it again the next week. Payment for the ads she sold would come in over the next month so my diet was still a lot of beans. But I coped and, like Scrooge McDuck, I dreamed of my very own a filthy lucre vault someday.

Chapter 25

That roll top desk later played another important role in the business—that of keeping the owner (me) out of therapy. After a few years, the board of directors, Andy, Carolyn and I, decided to reward Eileen for her diligence, successful sales pitches, and ability to keep us schlepping along. To our pleasant surprise, we later learned she had turned down some astonishing offers from other newspapers to stay with the Editions. (A mini miracle?) She liked working with us! And she loved that desk.

Before she might take another better offer we bought her a new, modern desk with (hey, get this!) inlays. First class, Baby! Then I took the roll top home and began my therapy of refinishing old furniture (not antiques, per se—junk stuff we could afford that only needed minor restoration surgery and the "used junk" dealer was anxious to get out of his shop). I dreamily and thoughtlessly scraped, sanded, filled holes and jury-rigged the desk and it now sits proudly in my home office, a tasteful part of my remodeled 1920s era office. There were times when I needed some time to be thoughtless during those first years of "muckraking." Abusing wood will do that.

A good point for anyone to ponder; don't go home at night and fret about tomorrow's unpaid bills. Get a hobby where sleeping upright takes all your thought time. See, I didn't cry as much about the business when I was downstairs in my shop making sawdust. In fact, through the years I've therapeutically made several barrels of sawdust out of otherwise fine old furniture and it's a wonder I'm not on the EPA's most wanted list for oblivious polluting. I'm not a skilled restorer but I'm persistent and single minded, often enabling me to forget last week's editorial column in which I misspelled the President's name or some such faux pas. Once I started on a piece, I could make that wood scream in joyous exultation at becoming youthful,

new and beautiful again. Until it began to burn...
sometimes.

For hours perfectly harmless wood and I would
team up and nary a thought intruded about tribulation tempests ever came between us and our
dusty nirvana. Woes and begones were banished in
my workshop.

Right here I'll offer some additional sage advice
for anyone wanting to go into business for themselves, i.e. become a happy and successful entrepreneur. (That, incidentally, really means one who
can skip rope using only one hand.) Make sure
your hobby is such that won't cost you immoder-
ate emergency room visits, yet one that demands
concentrating so hard you won't think on how
to completely close your mind to avoid facing
responsibility.

I became a home handy man of immeasurable
skill. Never did learn to use a tape measure worth
a darn and that little inadequacy kept my proj-
ects going a big bit longer than expected—which
meant I had less time to speculate whether the
bank was going to renew my note.

One day when my lawyer wouldn't return my
calls, I decided I had to do something to get my
mind off things like sniveling and humiliation and

starvation and... I decided to repair an ornate picture frame. It saved me buckets of tears and frets. It even provided material for another column. In addition to my other duty-ducking methods, I found a way to play with the cat more often.

Why didn't I do that?

I think in peculiar ways. Not necessarily on purpose; more like: "Oh, fer cryin out loud, that was really, really stupid!"

We have this oil painting that is in a very ornate and extroverted frame. It's not a Renoir— bought it at a flea market—but we love it. The frame, though, is one of those old-fashioned ones with lots of globby scrollwork. I've agonized over spending gobs of money to restore the injured globs. Over the years, I've discussed it with restoration folks and all told me it was a very demanding task and would cost accordingly—like a triple bypass.

In a fit of distracted whimsy, I decided to do it myself. Bought some putty and artsy-like paint. Then I put everything in my shop for about two years while I worked up the audacity to attempt the probable annihilation of the frame. I'd look at the frame every fortnight or so and determine that next weekend I do it. Then I'd chicken out and pretend the chips, missing putty and broken corners added its antique value. (Pretending the painting was valuable meant I could worry more about the taxes I'd owe once I refurbished the frame.)

Last weekend, I closed my mind, a simple task if you're a journalist, and mentally submerged my other frailties. I gingerly placed the frame on my workbench, looking ever more closely at the intricate scrollwork adorning this audacious wonder from some starving artist's inner turmoil. On closer inspection, I emitted an "I'll be damned," The thing looked like some guy stood back about 10 feet and threw plaster at the corners. Maybe the same guy filled a toothbrush with paint and flang it at the sides and then finger painted until dinnertime.

Not one beautifully sculpted corner was exactly like another. So that's how artists get away with it, I surmised. Creativity is pure luck and maybe a good pitching arm. However, as I pondered the whole from a safe distance, the corners looked perfectly matched. Uh huh! I stood back and whopped some putty at the traumatized corners, achieving a relaxed and balanced 90-degree angle with a sort of potbelly.

Then I put some red dye in the cat's food and waited the necessary three hours before carrying her down to the shop where I had my recorder set on LOUD with a recording of the neighbor's' dog barking. Aimed the appropriate cat end at the frame and turned on the recorder, and, I'll be darned, I had a restored frame. (I did have one bit of remission, though; I always wondered how artists did that. If they could make money at this easy task, why the heck are there so many stray cats?).

My restoration looks as accomplished as the original must have—if you squint...in the dark...through sunglasses.

While doctoring the cat scratches on my hands and stomach, I got to thinking about all the things we never notice until we put our nose to it. It's the perception of skill, not the finished product. All those things we never attempt because it looks too difficult. Well, sure, I learned to tie my shoes and can spell hypothetically *(def: making up reasons why you should never actually trust your third cousin once removed with your portfolio.) That's conjecturally why I never pursued my childhood dream of becoming a belly dancer— which I used to believe I'd be very good at until I learned that "belly" ain't necessarily the biggest attribute required.*

-30-

Of course there were moments when nothing could keep the thought process buoyant. There were times when one recession bloomed into another, when I got to thinking what if I fail as a publisher? What else could I possibly do with my limited intellectual bent? Or in more weepy moments, what can I do with the talents I possess? Things were getting pretty grim about now, and I got to thinking about the simplest vocation of which I could conceive. I could think of only one job that I couldn't possibly fail.

In high school, when a grumpy music director discouraged me from playing a 12-string guitar, I caved... No. Wait. That doesn't count. He was right. Thing is, we're not all cut out to play a guitar like Chet Atkins, brave enough to be an astronaut or slim enough to dance exotically. But, by dang, how we gonna know if we don't take a fling at it?

Remember all those times you've read about someone who wrote a best seller or invented a new way of cooking bacon without burning it and you told yourself, "I coulda done that!" How about all those seminars you've attended, admiring upon that self proclaimed expert up there giving you perspicacious advice on how you, too, could be svelte if you don't eat chocolate cake? You already knew that but you paid to hear it, didn't you, you wimpy non-achiever?

How come you and I never became a wealthy luminary or an expert charging hefty fees to lecture others on things we already know but were afraid to admit we were too cautious to try? It's because we think "they" know what they're doing and "they" know we know that but as long as we're willing to buy their book, they'll keep giving us "The Annotated Scholarly Works of Rambo."

We must learn to have faith. The only real complication in life is, why do many (not all) folks with limited intellectual bent become leaders, experts, celebrities and really rich retired politicians? Well, shoot, they just didn't know better, so they did it.

So get out there and make a rich fool of yourself.

If I could've sold ads, I'd have made Eileen publisher, editor, news writer, deliverer of Editions and CEO of the bathroom. She was from our hometown of Loveland. Although she was a bit younger than Carolyn and me, we had known her family when we were growing up and I knew she came from good stock. I gave her a crash course in selling ads (Go knock on doors and plead). That was about the limit of her "orientation."

I couldn't sell a $100 bill to a to a homeless person for two bits, so I had to sit back and watch her increase her income to what the activists would deem unfair wages (she later told me she took the job because she needed an extra $50 a week for household expenses. Oh, Lord, had I only known…) while Carolyn and I signed her checks as I dreamed about where the next blessing might come along.

It took me a long time to get over my envy (and downright disgust) of Eileen, probably about the time her gross sales went up to $100,000 a year. I had to admit she was our "bread and butter" and I had to swallow my pride for the first few years while ensuring she got paid before the office rent and the web press folks who printed our whimsical attempt at informing the public who more often than not had already been newsily inundated by the dailies, TV news and the Internet. Those were not prideful days for me, but Eileen more than made up for it later. She made it almost feasible for me to buy a Buick Regal, a luxury car to one supporting an old Ford pickup whose power steering was me. And I've blessed her for it for 30 years.

Love that lady.

But…miracle of miracles again, Eileen turned out to be a workaholic—not only to her advantage, but certainly to the Editions.

It made me grumpy to suspect Eileen probably was making some stockbroker very happy. I started to rationalize every time I had the urge to fire her. But instead of firing her and hoping she'd lose money in the stock market, I wrote whiney editorials and columns full of excuses as to why I was not getting wealthy. I rationalized that my turn would come, maybe through the lottery or that nice man from Libya who had stolen $30 million he had to launder and needed my bank account number soonest.

I think I was searching for pity when I wrote the following column.

> *It's how you look at it*
> *You ever get one of those phone calls from these folks who tell you, "If you had invested $10,000 when you were 25, you'd be a millionaire today?"*

I didn't have ten grand to invest when I was twenty-five. Like most people at that stage of life, I bought my toothpaste on the layaway plan.

People who tell me how successful and wealthy I could have been if only I'd… make me wanna puke. Every day I realize how numb dumb I was, am and will be just because financial security was only a grossly, successful, filthy profit just out of my reach if I hadn't fallen asleep at the investment seminar.

Now that I'm approaching maturity, I don't want to be reminded of what could have been, dang it! I'd rather not recall flunking my high school Home and Family Living class because if I'd passed, I might have become a highly overpaid butler.

We all know someone who has a story like the Polaroid one, where if they'd put fifty bucks into Mr. Land's gadget camera, they'd be swimming with the dolphins in the Caribbean. Or that fella Walt Disney who's crazy idea to build a carnival in LA would have made their $500 investment make Microsoft's Bill Gates at least give a knowing nod when he walks by me in the Five-Star restaurant.

A fella once offered me half interest in a $10,000 Vail, Colorado condo. I sniffed and snickered at his foolishness until a few years later he sold it for $100,000. Then there's the old classmate who joined the Secret Service and later wrote a take-off on the book, "I Led Three Lives." He called his, "I Told Three Lies," an unauthorized biography of a certain Congress Person. He asked me to ghost write it but it was only after I'd turned him down I learned he'd received a publishers advance of $2 million—with which he later bought an abused S&L.

It's foolish to always wish things had turned out differently. Like the guy in the saloon the other day bemoaning the fact that he wasn't born a flat-chested girl. "Geez, I coulda got a silicon implant and I'd sue and be rich today." You figure it out.

As you get older and the opportunities get harder to amortize, the best thing is to pretend the sour grapes are not really that bad. Like the time my father-in-law offered to sell me the back forty acres of his dairy farm when he retired. I didn't take him up on it and now I'm glad. See, today that back forty must have a hundred homes on it. Can you imagine all the fuss and bother I saved myself, what with not having to obtain all those building permits while finding an honest real estate agent to handle all those complicated sales. Oh, the headaches of those tortuous tax returns. Or how about trying to keep the kids happy when it was time to divide the estate? I am a lucky guy.

Maybe we waste too much of our lives dwelling on what might have been. We oughtta learn to retain only the good memories. Once I bought some stock, kept it for about five years and sold it. Made enough money to buy Carolyn a very nice dinner. It later went up…well, you know the story. I remember it was a pretty good dinner. Always search for the intellectually flawless validation; it means there will be fewer times you wrench your back while kicking yourself.

I was just telling Carolyn the other day, right after the $300 million lottery drawing, that it's a good thing I didn't buy a ticket because the winning numbers obviously were sold to someone else. I bought a cup of coffee with the dollar I saved.

Sages of the ages will tell you that's how to delude yourself into happily enjoying your Golden years suckling on Social Security—unless you are one who learns to recognize a miracle for what it is.

-30-

Chapter 26

So, the newspaper was now launched now that we had an editor/writer, me, an office manager, Carolyn, and a sales lady, Eileen. "What next, Don Quixote?" I asked my muse.

It occurred to me about the second week (we were three weeks away from publishing the first edition of The Cheyenne Edition) and a small problem arose in my entrepreneurial mind. If I have a paper with stories and ads in it, how do I get it produced and printed?

I called a gentleman who was running a weekly newspaper in one of the suburbs. We made an appointment and I asked him about his system. And then I asked could I pay him to help me put out the Editions? He, seemed a bit reluctant, but agreed to show me the way and let me use his type-setter machine thingy and his layout man to paste up out our newspaper. For about eighteen months, the crew (Eileen and I—Carolyn had to stay at the Editions office to take messages, hoping for the story of the century) traveled to Manitou Springs every Thursday morning to paste up the paper.

I learned later why the fella was hesitat-ing to deal. He had been planning a newspaper in the same neighborhood I had glommed onto about six months before his planned launch. Was that another miracle? Would I have started the Cheyenne Edition if another newspaper was already there? Would Don have asked me to provide him with an advertising source if another newspaper was already there? Are cats ever contrite?

By now I was paying closer attention to what was happening outside my own body and brain, that there might be more to life than my IQ would willingly allow admittance. Or was I maybe detect-ing more providential coincidences occurring these days? I mean, good luck just doesn't happen in bunches—unless there is some scheme at work. Was something else giving aid to an extremely ill equipped dreamer of dreams? I was tempted to look over my shoulder for a fairy godmother and when I finally did, look, I got a large case of the shudders. Didn't find my FG but there was something out there, y'know. It was the beginning of the life of a believer.

Soon something else happened. Our eldest son, Andy, finished his "artsy" welders' trade school training on how to build fancy porch rails and such, and was back home again. While he was looking for a job, he hung around the newspaper office. I put him to work doing things I didn't want to do, figuring if he was going hang out, live at home, and expect us to feed him, by cracky, then he could earn his way.

As time went by, he took over setting up newspaper carrier routes and… You know, I don't remember much else he did in those days. I kept asking him how the job hunt was going and he mumbled a lot of teenage talk—which I still don't understand (a skill our grandchildren have made worse, especially as I now hear more slowly).

The weeks, then months, went by and Andy kept coming to the news office; before long he was working most days all day long. And it stayed that way for a couple years as he tasked himself to learn how you laid out a newspaper for the press run.

(That's when you paste the waxed newsprint to the grid sheets so that the press could take photos of them and put the photo negatives onto this big, noisy, two-story high contraption and start the press to run off our wonderful little newspaper. I hope the above job description doesn't confuse you as it still does me.)

The old ways of putting out a paper were more intensive than today. Sharpening all those quill pens and putting ideas down on papyrus seemed to soothe me in some bewitching way. Now, though, we had to worry over days when the computers at the press would "go down" just as deadline was approaching and you knew you're were going to have only dandelion casserole and nuts stolen from the squirrel nests next week if you didn't get a paper out because your advertisers will refuse to pay you because their ad didn't get out that week. Oh, the very existence of a small business owner can be cruel. It wasn't our fault but the advertisers didn't care! Business is business unless you are a hermit in Krasnoyark, Siberia.

About two or so years later, Andy walked in one morning and suggested we do the carrier lists on a computer. I knew they were using computers to design Saturn rockets at NASA, but I felt we didn't have the money for that kind of intense spending. And besides, computers were for people who didn't want to face that real work made the man.

He quickly set me straight. For only about two months' income, we could set up a computer "slave" system and really save time and money and whiteout. (I learned later that computers are not slaves any more than are public servants.)

Two months' income for a box with a green screen that fantasiously makes squiggles more efficiently than good old-fashioned, sweaty-nosed typesetting? Hey, I wanted to learn from my mistakes, but not to the extent that I had to worry about a grey box on my desk that might out think me at any moment. Computers, I avowed, were used only by people with PhDs and other hot shot lazy slackers writing poetry for some communist cause or other.

Andy laughed 'cause he knew ol' dad lived by "that's the way we always did it." High tech was not of my tried and true world. To tell how far I was from being forever cursed by a "delete" key, the first thought in my mind was where would he put a computer in our little office? Those huge Univac computer thingies printing all those holy-holed cards I'd seen in the movies filled a room larger than our office, even if we included the next door restaurant.

It was a evil, grungy day when I walked into the Cheyenne Edition office and found a big grey chunk of plastic sitting on a desk–right in the middle of the office where, if I'd had any friends visiting, I'd have had to explain what was going on and I didn't have any frivolous remarks prepared to prove that I knew what was going on. How to explain this machine to my peers? I know I'm old fashioned but computers never need oiling nor do they need gears. Actually computers just might be close to a secular miracle of communication but I'm not yet ready to admit they are a perpetual motion evolution; they don't have any moving parts that can be replaced when a stoppage occurs! Besides, people seem to think editors know everything and I wasn't ready to disabuse my friends of my worldliness.

I'd heard that computers crash! What if someone was standing beside it when that urge came? Would we get sued? Or powerful enough to knock out a wall? Chipping away at your sense of well-being. Byting my muse. Why, I'd even heard that people actually quit thinking once they got a computer, which meant there would soon be people unable to take seriously my newspaper columns.

This thing they were calling the great leap to a CPU (that's supposedly the brain of the machine which, if you think about it, the Great Apocalypse takes on a new meaning) that would haunt middle managers in big companies who would soon be cursed with stress trying to keep the peasants busy. This computer thing was not only going to save trees—they didn't need paper—they would change the earth's atmosphere so much that in a few years it was going to be globally hot all the way around! I knew I wasn't ready for this but I didn't want to appear to be not taking advantage of the cutting edge of technology or inhibiting my child. I capitulated. And, I was curious.

Soon, Andy was sitting at this monster model of lost initiative, working away like an eldest son is supposed to. I timidly asked what he was doing, knowing I'd better be ready when our wickedly astute and frugal accountant walked in and asked "What's that?"

But here's Andy trying to explain to his dad who is absolutely ignorant of DOS (I had a lot of "duhs" to overcome), and completely innocent of what this "word processing" fickleness could do to a normal human being's id. (I was cursed by my own timid acquiescence, which marked the end of my contented world of learning from past blunders and, I believe, led to new blunders which then led to the need of new miracles. I was not, as you have probably surmised, a fast learner. I was exceedingly exorcized by the specter of copelessness.)

It was a traumatic episode in my life as a publisher. I felt as if I was leaving the world I loved. I saw "Star Trek" and Darth Vader did not look like someone with whom I wanted to get acquainted. Still, I vowed to master this new medium because I had no idea what they'd done with my faithful Royal, which mysteriously went the way of the ribbon the next day. I did get a bit of revenge a couple years later with this "I told you!" column.

> *My cup sprung a leak*
>
> *It was just a couple years ago that the staff stole the ribbon from my 1927 Royal typewriter (the one with the windows on each side—a valuable antique of incalculable worth but they don't make ribbons for it anymore). It was their way of telling me they would put up with my pale prose no longer.*
>
> *Then they put a computer on my desk.*
>
> *Now, I loved the way those Royal keys would go clackity-clack, sort of a lusty resonant melody, y'know, as I punched out wisdomly gems worthy*

of being embedded with the work of lesser known prose positing pretenders. I really hated to give up that old companion; it was a gift from a friend. Well, he was going to throw it away and I stole it from his car.

Over the years we'd formed a comfortable companionship; it couldn't spell and I couldn't write a straight line. Between us, we hacked out adverbs and nouns, dangled participles, plodded to predicates and numbed our readers with non-sequiturs. I loved its platen.

These high tech bytes and RAMS were a passing fad, I adjudged, destined to go the way of other new fangle-like l-e-d whims, like the Titanic and bell-bottom double-knit saggy butt trousers. No serious writer really believed a hard-hitting story or column could be written without hitting hard on a made-by-a-real-human steel keyboard. Only wimps and sensitive facilitators were satisfied by that tippity-tappity, pardon-me-plastic computer keyboard that sent an R into the air to supposedly reappear—get this—on a green screen that sits remotely self-important somewhere else on your desk. C'mon!

Hey, with my Royal, you got what you got, right there on paper you could crumple, wad and throw, in black and white, red if you were ticked off. You whacked the H and by damn there it was! No apology needed. With these word processors, (sounds like timid impertinence, don't it?) you can't "whack" anything out; the best you can get is a dainty dab at suggestiveness. Great reporters like Damon Runyan would have giggled.

But anyway, the staff convinced me to go high tech, promising I'd learn to esteem the way my words would magically whiff though the ether and blessedly resuscitate on that absentee screen. And, of course, I would become a much better writer, what with spel chek, automatic tabs, headers… floppy discs…and lots of ctrl and alt—cursors.

Now I'd writ for years using cursors but to prevent a lockout, I capitulated, not knowing there were dangers inherent, lurking and waiting for an old coot who can't think when his finger's got a blister. They didn't tell me about CRASH! Or ABORT! ERASE! Or why "Belgian Franc" was part of the program that popped up just as you were searching for that one consecrated key that will save your Homeric rhetoric. No, sir, they didn't talk about that.

So, now I've written this epic column, one that will guarantee peace in our time, has phrases that

*will serve as an inheritance to numberless ante-
cedents across the decades. I'd been working on
this mystic but mighty masterpiece for hundreds
of Sunday mornings, faithfully noting on my
bedside notepad at three or four am, waiting for
its majesty to jell into coherence. It would have
explained* why *the Ten Commandments, platinu-
mized the Golden Rule, partitioned partisanship
and ruled Britannia while projecting a meaningful time for the Second Coming.*

It was that good.

*You know what happened? Sure you do.
There's this key, you see, that locks the keyboard,
the screen, the on/off switch, the toilet, your diges-
tive system and makes it rain on weekends. It's not
visible, this key, on the keyboard or in the massive
instruction manual. It has not been discovered in
ancient Egyptian hieroglyphics nor will it ever be
magnified by the Hubble spacecraft lens. It may
be somewhere in Revelations, but I don't think so.*

*The key struck. The column is gone. Experts
say it was probably a power surge that somehow
let the system reboot itself while I was changing the
subject. Ergo, the glorious aria of the ages is destined to become a non-entity in mankind's bounty*

because, I the Oracle of the Keyboard of HP, left the infernal machine untended to get a candy bar.

And now this miraculous computerized epiphany worshiped by the speaking world as the greatest communications force since drum rolls at a military execution will bring forth only this Richard Armour pithy ditty:

Shake and shake
The catsup bottle,
None will come and then a lot'll.

-30-

Indeed, progress must be progressive. The world must be improved by whatever means our scientists, doctors, trash collectors, activists can come up with; mostly government grants. I fully admit that computers will reinvigorate commerce, political campaigns and snow plowing in Minneapolis. I will faithfully keep searching for that corrupt key of the Devil's doing as my contribution to mankind's sustaining journey to complete pollution of the earth. But, and I'm serious now, I won't even think about such a project without some serious help from Above. I'm still learning how to not abuse blessings.

Chapter 27

Thus began a whole new world for the Walter Empire. One for which I was not psychically or mentally equipped. New horizons beckoned that I did not recognize; new ventures of which I was frightened, were messing with my adopted horizons and habits. One being, how did you wad up and throw the screen into the waste basket when you were dissatisfied with what you'd just written?

There were new friends who encouraged me during some dark computer-mastering attempts and some old friends who reminded me that at my age, the newspaper world might be my final fling at achieving self-respect. Anything was possible, so they said, sometimes with a straight face. The idea persevered in my mind. But hadn't a computer already terminally eliminated my column when I had turned my back? Hmm.

Those "tried and new" acquaintances' encouragement and counsel spurred me on through those early years at the new and wonderful Walter Publishing domain. At this time, I would like to make a statement that the business gurus don't usually offer to budding entrepreneurs: Listen to your friends. Decide early if the advice they are giving is toward what is possible or if it's hinting you are pursuing your dream sans the necessary "luggage", i.e., you may be under-qualified.

Then listen to the only one on this earth who knows you best (even if with some disapproval)—you. You may learn astonishing things about yourself. Do you have the perseverance to suffer the indignity of impecuniousness for years? Or will you walk away to find easier or healthier usage of your brainwaves? Have you the courage to unlock the office door on those days when you must speculate on how you are going to pay the rent? Will your computer respond to your supplications?

And most of all learn to recognize and count your blessings and discount your feelings of inadequacy!

If I learned anything, other than slowly coming to the fascinatingly bottomless suspicion that we are not alone, it was that anyone, me included, could do unexpectedly grand things just by pushing yourself to do a variety of tasks for the first time. If you pass those tests, then you must explore the possibility that you do, indeed, possess some gifts.

We determined our newspaper delivery day would be Friday. Actually, Thursday night was the only day the commercial press could squeeze us in. That first Thursday was a date that will live in persistency, to paraphrase a famous fellow. After a long day of wondering where this story should fit best or should that story be run, about seven pm, Carolyn and I carried our very first "flats" containing my dream to the big press in the north. We dropped off the flats and went home with what I felt was the rising of my first sun. We would go back to the press on Friday morning around eight am and pick up one hundred bundles of papers and take them back to our little office, count them and deliver each one to the driveways of the neighborhood.

That first morning, as the last of the Cheyenne Edition came off the press, I stood about fifteen feet away, marveling at what I had created. We had labored long and hard bringing to fruition our very first Cheyenne Edition, Volume I, Number I, dated January 29, 1982. I was so proud as I listened to the mechanical "heartbeat" of the giant press running off our newspaper as it thrum-thrummed right along with my heart. On the front page we had photos of some old little huts of long ago when tuberculosis sufferers came to convalesce in Colorado Springs' pure mountain air back around the turn of the century (20th, not 21st). There was a story about the Cheyenne High School's great showing on the "Preliminary Scholastic Aptitude Test (Headline #1—Cheyenne PSATs consistent rank tops nationally) on the front page, along with a story telling folks we were "open for business" with their brand new neighborhood newspaper.

I was so proud, I almost decided to take all the issues home and savor them into my dotage. But that would have self defeating. If those ads didn't get out to the readers in the neighborhood, my dotage might have been a bit grim.

There was just one problem. Overnight, Mother Nature had deposited about eighteen inches of snow in our delivery neighborhood. Drifts up to two feet! And just me and the boys, Andy, Peter and Nathan with a couple of their friends went forth to deliver 5,000 copies of my soul and body.

I had a 1968 Ford one-half ton pickup that held about half the first twelve-page newspaper bundles.

I wondered if God was sending a message. I watched as those young boys fought their way through those 24-inch snowdrifts to deliver those papers to the porches. They were from twelve to seventeen years old and my heart soared as I saw them struggle through snow up to their waists. Since Nathan was only about four feet tall, we all kept a close eye on him. I'm afraid I wasn't as worried about losing him as I was about getting the papers delivered.

It took us all day that Friday and half of Saturday to deliver those 5,000 copies. I dragged us all home to dry out, refresh and, for the boys, to take their first paycheck to the shopping center. Me? I headed for a hot shower and my easy chair and read and read and read the glory of my own creation. It was a moment I wished that everyone in the whole could have shared with me. I don't know if it was like giving birth, but the sensation made me feel as if I'd experienced a little bit of paradise.

We'd done it! Our newspaper was in the hands of our hope-they'll-be-enthralled readers. Would they read it? Would they rush right down to the stores and buy lots of things they'd just read about in our paper? Heaven forbid the copies end up as "weekly wipes," carpet for birdcages or sooner than later making the trash hauling companies wonder why the trashcans were so full that week?

When I arrived home late that first Saturday, I was already mentally calculating how many more Fridays left in 1982. At my advanced maturity level, I worried a bit over whether could I do this forty-eight more times? Yet I really had few choices: accept poverty, go back to being a productive citizen—or persevere, hoping my retrograde to the newsboy status of forty years ago would only be temporary and I would become a mogul.

I had timidly penned my first column which I hoped would lead to the first stage of long time communication between our readers and myself that might launch a new world order sans pestilence, wars and famine. I don't recall what erudite, glowing, guiding principles I espoused to ensure eternal serenity among my many fans-to-be. I called it "Observations." "Editorial" seemed so pompous at that early stage. I saved the pompousness for later exposition down the years.

Within weeks we began to hear back from our readers. Almost all positive except for a few warthogs that probably never even read their birth certificate. Things just hummed along for the next couple of years. Advertising sales began to equal survival needs at least two out of four weeks. Then suddenly they took off and I could shrug confidently to our banker when he dropped by, I suppose checking to see if we were still open.

There wasn't a plethora of diamonds and Rolex watch-type revenue pouring in, but word soon got around that the Editions newspaper might be serious about all this publishing and throwing papers around the neighborhood. As they say, word of mouth is the best advertising –at least at first— and sure enough, we soon began getting calls from folks wanting a share of our money; sales people, non-profits, consultants of all breeds. Mostly to "participate" in our good stewardship or those wanting to help us succeed in our publishing venture, but so many! I didn't know there were that many talented writers and consultants in our town.

Chapter 28

The very next week, the second of our miracle odyssey, another piece dropped out of the blue. Counting my blessings years later, I think I was beginning to realize something wonderful was happening. Joanna arrived on the scene. And what a "Scene" it became.

Joanna Fischer dropped by the Editions office and before tea time the "Cheyenne Scene" society column was born. Joanna is a very unusual person. She not only had the talent to write a "society column," she had the contacts and a wonderful, loving personality that enabled her to "magnetize" the doers and make-it-happen-socialites of the neighborhood and she soon had a stable of contacts for almost all civic activities in the whole darned county.

She was already involved with ninety percent of all the "happenings" and events of import in the Colorado Springs notable "500" club. She knew everybody and everybody who was anybody knew and loved her. What a gad-a-bout! What a "find!"

Soon this "little" neighborhood newspaper was the talk of the town. The big daily couldn't cover very much of the neighborhood news and Joanna knew the niches they were missing. She soon had every PR person in town calling in events that were important to our readership. Nobody admitted to reading her "social column," but we noticed that when Joanna covered an event and included lots and lots of names, our newsstands emptied pretty quickly on Friday afternoons.

Her column soon became the "place to look" if you wanted to find your name in the "upper" echelons of local standing. If you made the Cheyenne Scene, you were, indeed, made! In fact, on our fifth anniversary, the biggie daily sent its own social columnist to our little bash, and danged if she didn't write more kind words about the Cheyenne Edition than did Joanna. We knew we had arrived when ink in the daily chanted the virtues of our little weekly fish wrapper.

A couple years later we had a poll taken on the Edition. Joanna's column ranked the best for readership, something like 85 percent. Yes, folks do indeed read the "social column," albeit in the privacy of their bathroom or wherever.

Miracles draw the "easy money" peddlers; just like that national magazine contest million dollar winner draws phony investment offers. Flies to honey are lethargic compared to opportunists landing on a new business.

And of course, we began getting letters from varied and sundry "government officials" in Liberia offering us millions of dollars if we'd only help them get many more millions safely out of their country. To do this, all they needed was the "loan" of our bank account number—"for jus' few days, Meesta Walter"—to store their stolen fortunes (most, they would explain, was stolen from really bad guys in their country and subterfuge was required to keep the bad guys from taking it back). What nice folks to trust me with their treasury for even those critical few days. I've never forgotten that comradely gesture…it seemed we were now considered legitimate suckers in the eyes of the "big money" people.

The Prince of the hustlers was the salesman who was selling these 1,000 pound cameras for a very large, well known publishing camera company. He had decided we could save money by doing all our production work before sending the week's offering to the press. If we had one of those newspaper production cameras and shot our own negatives of our layout sheets, we could save something like $7.50 per page. Whooee, who wouldn't jump on that bandwagon?

The salesman, who was from Denver, showed up within forty-five minutes of his call, normally an hour's drive If the prospect didn't sound like a sitting duck. And, to make a long story readable, we bought the camera and a developing system that looked about the size of two refrigerators. I felt as if I taken another step toward professonalship as a publisher.

We tussled from day one to get that developer to work. First our classified advertising salesman convinced us he was a camera pro. Sadly, I didn't ask what sort of camera. The first Friday's production process went from early Thursday morning until early Friday morning. Of course, we missed our deadline at the press, but back then they were more reasonable. We were in a bull market.

Richard tried all danged night with the same sorry result. But those negatives still came out fuzzy and unprintable.

Struggle, you ain't never seen such an unfair contest. The thing just kept on eating negative paper without so much as an "excuse me" when it belched pages out. We just couldn't develop 'em up to newsprint quality.

The system didn't work. I mean, it did not work! It was like, since it was made in Italy, it refused to produce English. It turned out negative after negative that had not one readable word, photos that looked like a ghost story, and swirls and hieroglyphics oozing off its black face. Come around four am the next morning, we decided we had a problem. So Carolyn and I took the flats we'd been vainly trying to birth (that's the grid sheets to which we'd so delicately pasted our dreams) to the press and begged the experts there to finish the process. After assuring us of their majestic skill, this by the press foreman, Carolyn and I went to get some breakfast. The press did a marvelous job of deciphering our mosaic.

On Monday, I called the camera/developer salesman. I complained. I whined. I sobbed. I demanded expiation. To the camera company's credit, a couple suits showed up on Tuesday. They somewhat reluctantly slithered into our cellar dark room and under the scrutiny of their CIA-type flashlights, determined the rollers on the developer were almost worn out, and it was no wonder we couldn't get the stupid thing to work.

I opined that a brand new developer should not have worn rollers. The suits were baffled. This should not happen, they avowed piously. They represented a well established worldwide camera manufacturer that would be sorely embarrassed by the results Walter Publishing Company had achieved. Well, I considered us as least as important as their big old klutzy camera shop. I think they were patronizing me, but what the heck?

It was soul searching time. Finally, out of exhaustion and professional investigative astuteness, I turned to the salesman. "What happened?"

He looked at me with an expression of helplessness and offered this unique answer that could only have been approved by the United States Federal Board of Bureaucratic phlegm doctors: "You never said you wanted a *new* developer!"

There were several moments of shocked silence. I couldn't think of any retort that was adequate to demonstrate my wrath at what he'd wrought.

His superiors, the big wheels, could not believe anyone within their employment could be so dense as to reveal what may have been company procedure when dealing with first time customers.

And the soon to be unemployed salesman? He just stared into space and peed his pants.

The camera company agreed to take back the used—worn out—developer and the camera and refund our several thousand dollar investment in our future. We were so grateful, don't you know.

The hustlers and opportunists got the same word and quickly dialed our phone number. All kinds of offers started rolling in, from advisers who would show us how to avoid inept consultants, from other banks who simply knew our banker was not giving us all the help he should and offering great money saving ideas from *their* bank. From evangelists coming through town that would pray for our continued success if we'd come by and drop a little in the plate at that night's revival meeting.

And then there were those folks who had this deep feeling of concern for small business folks to whom they were giving the opportunity to buy their product. Products that would guarantee our continued success if we didn't read the fine print. AND they would "buy" an ad and continue to advertise, providing their ad brought in enough business before they had to pay for the ad. I soon became pseudo-cynical.

Our valiant "newsworthy" expedition went back to the old ways. There was a whole lot of waxing going on. You have to slather the back of all the typewritten stories. Then you wax the back of all the advertisements. Very carefully, now, each story and each ad must be laid on the layout sheet. If they are not straight, everyone in and out of the newspaper business would know we're a bunch of publishing pretenders and when your advertisers see their ad all kitty-wampus in your now-delivered newspaper, they will not laugh at your klutziness. No, indeed, they will not.

We started at eight am, laying out all the ads. Then we carefully placed the stories (editorial content, for you purists). I didn't learn for a decade or so the proper terminology for professional, competent, "Associated Press approved" publishing. Shoot, I believed if you got some interesting copy tucked between the paying ads, it was just a small step to bringing our "unique" publication to the forefront of fame and worshipful credibility. I would become known as "The Unlikeliest Newspaper Man" and whatever was within our sacred pages was worthy of the most strenuous mental consumption.

Through the months, the newspaper began to make a little money. Not a lot and it was disappointing when I learned that with even our meager profits, Uncle Sam still got a cut. (Later in life I learned that Uncle gets his cuts literally from cradle to grave. I've not yet found a pre-birth tax but a sage once told me The Congress is leaning toward legalizing cloning of children. There could then be a manufacturing fee levied on non mothers. That would be a pre-birth tax and it could well lead to an inventory tax.)

And there's that death tax thing, y'know, where even after you die the government is right there computing how much they'll charge the heirs in transportation costs to the next world. The biggest surprise I got was when I went on Social Security and learned that I have to pay taxes on my SS check. I declare, if government would put its expertise to work as effectively as it makes tax laws, we would have solved most problems before we knew they were problems. But government, whether it works well or not, usually produces bad news for the taxpayers. We need 'em but we can't afford 'em.

I've come to conclude that if there is a purgatory, there will be IRS agents there—on limited work visas, of course—with per diem—checking everyone out and setting up court dates for those dead people who left owing Uncle Sam an emigration tax. The agents don't waste much time with those folks headed for the nether regions; they would most likely tell those agents to come to hell anyway.

I do not want to lead you to suspect I am complaining. No sirree. There ain't many First World countries will allow private enterprise to tilt on the very edge of failure before they send the taxpayers a "stimulus package" by way of a U.S. Treasury check because we're too dumb to know how to protect ourselves from nannyism.

Less than trustworthy folks you might end up dealing with are actually a small part of the overall risk. The person who will help you the most, the one you must trust and listen to deeply is again, you. If you don't think partnering with yourself, whether you are a scalawag or a dim bulb, it's bad business and you might want to reconsider.

Mostly that's because you're stuck with yourself. Don't argue with you. Don't try to "snow" you. And for sure, don't give up on you. You know best the private reserves you have to draw on and you know your worst weaknesses.

One way I learned whether Hank Walter was a dependable guy or a dizzy dope with no visible skills was to sleep with him. In the darkness of midnight or three am, rolling and roiling on that uncomfortable bed, you'll soon learn, with the help of the Holy Spirit of course, if the two of you are a good match. Can you take the downturns with optimism and the upturns with frugalism? Yes? Then go see your banker.

You have now learned again Rule Number Several in starting a new business. If you want to be boss, don't whine when you face the ramifications. (By the by, I've never figured out which rule is more important. Therefore, all the tips I'm giving you for free are Rule Number One.)

Chapter 29

I suppose you're thinking, now that you've been farce-fed all the sage advice a retired curmudgeon can give; the most critical part of success is those around you. Well, yes, but there's more to beating the odds as a newly-birthed captain of industry. You could rank the next advice up there as number one; *money*, and you may be right. But without good people, it don't make no difference if you have all the money you need for the next ten decades.

And so, let's talk money. Friends, co-workers, advisers, even lottery wins, come and go. Money is the one thing you can always count on in business—but you have to have some to count. The flip side of that is learning to avoid bill collectors when you don your frogman's suit and dive into the deep, swirling waters of the always moving and unpredictable undertows of the business world.

I admit, when I went into business—both times—I was so broke I could ill afford any personal debt doubts. Sometimes I think being poor early on in life was another of those miracles. I didn't get hogtied by the payments for which I couldn't have afforded the insurance on a Corvette. My 1958 Ford pickup cleaned up very nicely.

The only real debt Carolyn and I had was our home mortgage and that turned out to be the most dependable financial asset coming to our rescue in hard times. We had a decent home equity so over the years our home (and mortgage holder) proved to be our best ally when time came to genuflect to the money lenders.

Some folks consider a mortgage as an apparition to be feared every first of the month. That's short-sighted of them. Your mortgage is your friend, steadier than rain in Seattle.

There is one caveat, however. Your mortgage is only as good as your diligence in taking care of the mortageed—your house. We all know some folks who couldn't use their residence as collateral for rock soup. They live in dumps of their own creation and neglect. I heard one banker say that looking at some folks "collateral" was more fun than the Comedy Club. (Sorry, but bankers are people, too. They need a sense of humor, even an unusual one.)

A small businessperson therefore has two obligations: Make money but if you don't, have a line of credit based on borrowing on your well-maintained home. A third option is to rent your wife out, guaranteeing she will do windows; not your best bet, however.

Sometimes after a sixteen- to twenty-three hour day at your very own dreamed-of snowshoe shop, it may seem a bit dispiriting to face house upkeep bills before going to bed, but do it. There were many times I just wanted to burn the house down rather than wash windows, but my strongest half (fear of failure, not Carolyn) made me do it anyway, including the windows that were stuck shut.

One must also learn to roll with the blow. Personal matters come second after making sure there's toilet paper in the john. A woe that took way too much of my professional mindset was brought upon my tired body not by normal maintenance chores. Woodpeckers! This episode in my life reminded me, in a way, of the old Alfred

Hitchcock movie, "The Birds." Only this time there was only one "victim"—my cedar siding.

You'll recall, I hope, my advice on keeping your house primo for the bank appraiser to look at. When we purchased our house so many years ago, I was not thinking of maintenance or a beautiful lawn. We liked the plan but, to my undying laborial gland's displeasure, we picked natural cedar siding. At that time we were out in the middle of the prairie and the nearest woodpecker was probably tearing down a distant rain forest. I had nothing to worry about.

But then...then, twenty years later I learned the folly of aging wood. Wood is not always good, as some armless lumberjacks will admit. Woodpeckers, though, have never run into a wood they didn't like. And so my wails of hopelesshood resounded through our quiet neighborhood when the woodpeckers used their squatters' rights. I wailed in print again. By the way, I do not consider this episode a miracle. Far from it; I almost got sued by the animal lover's league before I finally learned woodpecker language for "Off Limits." I stuccoed the house before my next loan review was due.

What's the number of the Homeowner's Protection Agency?

Is there a Human Protection Agency? I need help and the EPA won't call me back. They're busy trying to get Denver to spend maybe $5 million to uproot five or six homeowners and re-route E-470 because a Golden Eagle haughtily built a nest near the proposed highway.

Okay, people aren't scarce yet and eagles are. But what about birds that disrupt people nests? My house is under siege by woodpeckers. I have knotholes in my wood siding and for the last two years, these flipped out peckerbills must have decided it's the state's biggest tree. They peck out the knotholes, fluff up the insulation and make themselves to home. Soon it'll be on to diversity and, you got it, they'll be inviting squirrels and maybe small bears to cohabitate. Or they'll be drilling through the inner walls into my closet where I do my major cogitating.

Ever crafty, I devised a way to convince the peccant peckers that I'm one of those stealthy bigots so prevalent here in Colorado Springs. I waited until they were out eating endangered insects or attacking neighborhood dogs and toddlers and

I nailed patches over the pecked-out knotholes. House looks like those photos we see of Afghani post bombing raid homes, but when the woodpeckers came home, I figured they'd get the message and move to a more open-minded neighborhood. Didn't work.

The hard-headed hammerers knocked out the patches! One even, I swear, pecked out the adjoining knothole and set up a real estate office. Every time another woodpecker would fly by, he waved a little real estate sign and, dang it, in a week I had the ultimate rap group scrabbling about in my walls.

Cleverly, I bought some of that goop in a can that expands to fill holes. Being latently humane and not wanting to end up with some very foul fowl in my walls, I first tied a string on the cat's harness and attached her to the roof. Kind of let her swing in the wind, y'know, a sort of a mobile neighborhood watch. While they were outside busily trying to fricassee the cat, I ran up the ladder and swooshed in the goop.

Had an unexpected side effect because that night I got to worrying: What if a really stubborn momma woodpecker had hunkered down in there and I swooshed her to a heavenly perch?

For weeks, as I wallowed in nocturnal guilt, I restlessly pictured that momma rustling around, fighting vainly to escape her goopy prison, knowing she'd never raise an egg to puberty. I'm sure it was PC guilt, but my serenity was disrupted for days. (Oh dear, you don't suppose she really was in there?)

That was last year. I was finally reacquiring my torpid tendencies sans ghostly visions of a gasping bird crying, "Nevermore, Nevermore." Then came spring and danged if the woodpeckers didn't come back. They pecked out the dried goop and moved back in. I think they mean to fight it out this time. When I was mowing the other day, all along the lawn next to the house is littered with insulation. They'd thrown it out and moved in deeper.

My sympathetic doctor who looks for ways to lower my blood pressure, suggested birdshot— best when the neighbors are away. He thought Election Day would be good, when everyone will be at the polls voting out the incumbents. I can't wait that long. By that time the President will have another tax on ammunition and I won't be able to afford the shells. If it ain't one thing…

My helpful neighbor suggested I pour salt on their tails, capture them and dump 'em out on the prairie. Didn't work. When I knocked on their little holes, they just threw insulation at me and crawled deeper and I couldn't get both the shaker and my hand through the hole at the same time.

As I was falling off the ladder I saw dear neighbor rolling around on his lawn and holding his sides. I figure either I needed a smaller shaker or he'd gotten even for the time my carpenter ants got loose and ate his dog house.

I know the EPA has this Eleventh Commandment that if the fauna was there first, we are behooved to rearrange our lifestyle to accommodate them. But when my house was built, there wasn't a tree within two miles. So the question is who has imminent domain? If it's me, will it be tacky if I invite the guy next door to Thanksgiving dinner with an entree of "imported miniature turkeys" from Thailand?

-30-

Chapter 30

Before I give any more Number 1 rules, I must add one more miracle; one that snuck by me. One day while thinking over the problems and tribulations of effectively running a business, an odd feeling came over me. The things I worried about hadn't happened and didn't look like they were going to. Right there I knew. I had experienced the miracle of faith. I was really believing God was with me, carrying me. There was no message, just a sudden acceptance. How had I missed it?

At this time it is necessary to state Rule Number One for the third or fourth or… time. I'm not keeping track and neither should you. Every good rule in business, sooner or later, becomes important unless you've already changed your mind. Rules are hard to categorize. They all seem to start with "don't."

Is not paying your employee's withholding tax worse than not paying your employees? That's a rule you'll only break once because if you do it just one teeny time, your Uncle Sam will send you a reminder along with an ill-fitting suit with a big P on the back. As you progress in your occupation, you'll find some rules that used to be significant are no longer. Eight hours sleep, for instance, will lose its importance because its absence gets less noticeable through practice. And practice you will if you're going to make a profit before your epitaph is published.

You must learn to trust yourself, protect your collateral and laugh at your banker's jokes. (Work on that last one. They're not all about widders and orphans in distress. Like lawyers, bankers' jokes told on themselves are seldom humorous. That may be because neither profession provides a lot of laughs.)

You will also learn (maybe the hard way) that paid consultants often are overpaid even if all you do is buy them a cup of McDonald's too-hot coffee. Right off the top here, I'll admit everyone knows a good consultant. It's the bad ones you don't know that will heavily tap your wallet once they've told you everything you already knew but it's too late to back out because you already signed the contract.

No one really knows how many consultants ply their trade with absolutely no real world experience in what they're consulting over. Many consultants have studied and learned but never practiced and then retired to pass on their borrowed expertise. Some, however, are those who failed at managing hamburger house franchises.

It's hard to figure which is which and might be making all that advice up as they go. For the small businessperson, my advice is to avoid consultants until your accountant has threatened to put you on a pay-as-you-go basis and he or she refuses to take any more newspaper back issues to place in his bird cage. And then advance cautiously. I once hired a newspaper consultant and found out later he was a heavy equipment operator who operated "from the seat of his pants." It showed.

Just make sure the consultant you hire doesn't spell his or her vocation as "cunsoltint."

As I was facing withdrawal from the publisher's chair, I naturally tried to think of the best way to avoid work. I listened to my own advice for once and I couldn't think of any vocation more simple and less tiring than that of a weathered old coot well versed in blarney. If you're wondering how consultants get their start, I did some research before I retired at seventy.

(I almost didn't retire, you know. Went to the doctor to get a physical before I let go my insurance. He told me I had the heart of a forty-year-old. Pleased, I went to the dentist to have a checkup and he opined I had the gums of a sixteen-year-old. About two weeks later, I got a letter to the editor commenting on my latest column accusing me of having the mind of a six-year-old. Evidence seemed to suggest I was much too young to retire. Wouldn't have except I discovered Social Security would pay me more than my salary at the newspaper.) I stayed on for another five years.

Getting back to consultants, my looming retirement sent me into a spin of anticipation. I could be anything I wanted now that I didn't have to work for a living. Read on.

Retirement consultations
I pondered powerful last week as I helped Andy and Carolyn heft almost 25,000 Editions into the delivery van. Maybe I was ready to challenge

retirement, I thought. I had not known that one of the curses of retirement is that everything gets heavier and time passes more quickly, sometimes faster than you can enjoy a moment of regularity.

So, being a disciple of lethargism, I mulled and culled my destiny choices. Had to discount a few options. F'rinstance, I don't think I want to go into politics after hanging up the old pica pole. Carolyn has been making up my mind for years. Saying "yes, dear" to your "superior" is a lot easier than how I didn't do it…whatever the question. Had I gone into politics I wouldn't be faced with such demeaning answers. A pol would have explained it's not in the budget and the problem is solved.

Then I thought about joining the NBA… except…well, it's not so much that I'm staturely a low draft pick; my dribbling expertise is limited to when I sleep with my mouth open.

My dream of becoming an Irish tenor faded quickly (Tiny Tim was my role model). No, it was more that I'm a beer baritone and when I recently hit a fairly high note in the church choir, a kind soprano nudged me and suggested I should lose my microphone because I sounded like a magpie that swallowed a killer bee.

I was "oh, dearing" about what would become of me after I gave up my executive chair when it hit me. I could be a consultant. I'm already qualified: I can write confusedly; I seldom have an original idea; and I'm not reluctant to borrow someone else's ideas and then charge a hefty fee for unverifiable haphazard information.

Yes! *I'm gonna get some business cards printed. Then I'm gonna contact all the government agencies I can think of and help them find qualified executive managers. Just read about a school district paying a consultant $138,000 to find them a new exec. Now, what a consultant does is put help wanted ads in all the trade papers and if anyone calls him to apply, he "qualifies" them. ("Can you spell PTO?"), stuffs their resume into an envelope and mails it to the school district. Of course, the school board still has to interview and decide on the size of the guaranteed severance in case the new executive brags about his insider trading skills while on duty. But hey, the school district didn't have to pay for a help wanted ad. Make that point in your first job interview as a consultant.*

And you thought those ads telling you how to make thousands of dollars a day by stuffing envelopes were a scam, didn't you?

The best consulting is that sort which gives aid and confusion to the largest number of people while roundabouting a conclusion. And I have it. Remember the controversy over toilet paper a few years back? Whether the paper should roll off the top or the bottom?

I have the answer. (And for this advice, I could charge almost any government agency ten grand a day.) If you are tall, the paper should be mounted so that it rolls off the top. If you are short, it shouldn't.

Sounds pretty conclusive, eh? Not yet, my friends. There's a however *to be massaged. If you're lanky but slouch when you are seated, then the paper should roll from the back to conveniently come out on the bottom. However, what if you are, uh, sorta condensed in staturely mien, but also proud and sit up straight just like your third grade teacher told you to? Yup, over the top where you can reach it without falling off.*

Now I'm ready to bank my fees, right? Nyet. An amateur consultant would stop right there. But the nimble adviser will extend the billings by introducing social responsibility. Drag in recycling. Greening responsibly. The consummate consultant will insinuate that using toilet paper is…uh, wasteful. Ergo, equate the ecological properties of faxes vs. the old-fashioned use of corncobs that, in the end, will only scratch the surface of the original study, thereby resulting in a new consulting contract to explore the relative merits of fax contusions vs. fax ink infection. (I can now add "facilitator" to my portfolio.)

THAT is why consultants are handsomely paid. He/she strategically throws in a what-if now and then, tactically stretching the study with nuances mixed with civic duty. Add a few innocuous but non culpable facts and never, ever give a comprehensive answer. Because if you reach a conclusion, the fees stop.

Wait a minute here. Did I just get consultants mixed up with environmental lawyers? Hoo ah! Now I can charge a simultaneous attorney fee.

Now, where did I put my calculator?

-30-

Good advice can come from the four winds. The hints from your guardian angel are good, too, but then, most of us don't listen to the wind. Anyway, you never can be sure if it's just a blowhard or a tornado of useful gems to be absorbed on your way to becoming a slave to your business—which is umpteen times better than laboring as a slave for your congressman.

Listen to your elders. There is a plethora of old-fashioned advice that relates to the old and new world. Some lessons are eternal and it makes no difference what century it is. One thing is for sure: Your elders usually have more money than you and most times don't act as superior as a loan officer. Flatter them.

I realized early on that telling the truth when something went awry or is going amiss is as cost-effective today as it was when Noah was filling out the animal manifest. I doubt Noah felt the urge to cook the books when he told the Lord how much feed he'd need.

Noah had an advantage. He knew with whom he was dealing. Would you believe that is a good habit to form? You never really know, for sure and specifically which life-force you are dealing with but anyone can tell you it's better to go with the odds. Esar's law (I don't know who he was either) says, "Pick a winner. Anyone can pick a loser." I accepted God as my partner.

Senior citizens have made it to that Golden age by doing something right during their productive years while aspiring to become wise old fogies. They may now tell the same stories over and over, but if you listen politely and closely, you may pick up that one priceless phrase or idea that makes you a millionaire—or a masseuse, if that's what you want. Or not. Remember, trying to understand and accept "gray hair experience" is hands-on and real time, and a lot better than your chances if you waste a buck on a lottery ticket. Listen to that older voice. For a leg up, especially listen for one that seems to come out of nowhere.

Chapter 31

Don't ever begin to think success is all about you. If you did it *your* way, you may have been just plain lucky. Luck, though, can be a fair weather friend. Luck is that partner that will pack its bags when the economy goes into a Barf market. Or is that Bear? The neat thing about miracles is they don't depend on the stock market.

This is a good time to remind you of all the things that can happen despite you. There will come a time when you've achieved a modicum of success and you're beginning to precariously believe you are the one who's put this all together, how valuable you've been to the achievements you've somehow attained. Cockiness begets over-confidence. Overconfidence begets penury.

Don't be like that. Wait ten years after you've consistently paid the bills on time before you boast what a good boy you are. You start exhibiting prematurely what a splendid business specimen you are and you'll sure as shootin' soon end up employeeless. That can be extremely detrimental to your entrepreneurial whimsies. Resist acting like a hot dog, bragging about how successful you are. Don't buy that condo in Hawaii or hire a butler to hang up your tuxedo before you get rich enough to hire a come-to-your-office manicurist.

Don't put your pelf into unproved possibles. Possibles can quickly turn into predicaments—like insolvency. Now's the time to kick back and consider what got you here. How many miracles you didn't recognize that may have influenced your decisions when you just thought you were guessing right?

And for sure don't ever forget that those working with you had just as much or more to do with whatever personal success you might likely be ready to claim. They can be one of that string of miracles I've been talking about; they're hard to recognize as you are signing those paychecks that anemic-ize your own salary. Miracles can take more faces than a Hollywood actor at a political rally. A good person giving you an honest day's work is hard to find. The last couple generations have been taught they are number one and, if for some unplumbed reason they find that they are not, they must be victims.

Another reason for charting miracles is they not only encourage you to trust better times are coming, they provide a "meanwhile" comfort zone that is out of this world. If you're smart, you'll soon come to know there is a Mentor who will never leave you by yourself. That ain't just fact. That's faith, brother, and when you recognize that, you'll sleep better. And work smarter.

My empirical experience of knowing many very successful folks is that many are not overly happy and some are downright cantankerous. Sure they made money but the cost of piling up dollars at the expense of compassion for your coworkers is too often higher than an IRS penalty and interest notice.

I still wasn't recognizing or counting on miracles when the bright idea of launching a second newspaper tickled my super ego. We'd made money for about two years with the Cheyenne Edition. So I talked myself into thinking it had been easy. What point was there in waiting any longer to launch a second money maker? I mean what with my newly acquired talents of three whole years as a shrewd publisher, what could go wrong?

Everything!

In 1985, I launched the Sand Creek Edition newspaper in a less affluent area just to the east of the Cheyenne neighborhood. Although I'd done my marketing research in Sand Creek and had gotten advertising commitments from several businesses, I'd missed the economic signals hinting that a recession was in the making. Or maybe I was ignoring them.

At that time in life I wasn't reading the Wall Street Journal or suffering the bulls and bears of the stock market. Mostly, it was the comic strip "Katzenjammer Kids" and the sports pages, which may explain why I strived mightily upstream when the already contracted buyer of the biggest ad commitment from a hardware chain closed its doors soon after the first issue of Sand Creek. Then another... and another...and by the end of the first year in Sand Creek, I began to notice I was paying the S.C. employees out of my insufficiently deep pocket.

Once again I'd gone into debt for the Sand Creek and it had cost me about nine and a half times what I'd splurged on the Cheyenne Edition. You may ask why so much more? I'm not embarrassed to say

I don't have any idea. Inflation? More employees? More copies of the Sand Creek? Or maybe it was just paying off the bank loan at a higher percentage rate than the C.E. loan.

Sadly wiser, I closed the Sand Creek, paid off my investment partner and settled down to write an explanation to the banker why I would not be spending quite so much money now. The thing now was to concentrate on the Cheyenne Edition and keep smiling.

It might have been the specter of a customer puking while visiting his office, but the banker renewed my loan. The lesson learned? Unlike digging a hole, it takes much longer to refill your bank account unless you have a lot of dirt to declare as collateral.

Oh, all right, I'm here playing with my father's bankers' reputations as mean, money-grubbing lovers of pelf. Every good book needs some threatening drama, don't you know. Don is a wonderful gentleman who gave me a lot of advice—but no more money—on how to recover solvency and still get a sense of pseudo extravagance by putting Jack cheese on my Spam sandwich. He also promised to let me know ahead of time when the loan committee was going to meet so I could be out of town when they wanted financial explanations. Don must have been a real whiz at convincing the committee of my "real" worth, although he never bothered to tell me what it was. Probably too complicated for an entrepreneur, anyway.

You know what, though? I was ahead of the game. The loan committee knew they wouldn't get diddly if I was forced to close the C.E. So it was a simple matter of them paying close attention to my silhouette—watching that I didn't flirt with starvation. More to the point, I'm pretty sure they didn't want to be surprised after I'd spent all the petty cash on a last magnificent supper at the Broadmoor Penrose Room.

As for Carolyn and me, we accustomed ourselves to look for any roadside kill on the way home from work on those days when we had a hunch the neighbors were tired of sharing their beans, taking weekend vacations in dumpy little towns within hitchhiking distance and staying in quaint little motels just across the street from the magnificent city dump right next to the WWII weapons demolition plant. That style of living is a marvelous way to control egos.

But when everything comes tumbling down at one whoop, it's harder to rationalize, thereby becoming tangibly unbearable. Or to put it more rationally, if you're starving by degrees, it's easier to believe you've still got a chance at financial recovery and you don't get discouraged as quickly as, say, a tsunami washes all your printers ink away. Watching your diet disintegrate helps avoid the whoops, too.

I've probably refinanced my home four or five times since the Sand Creek went dry. But since every rejuvenation of faux courage (using the bank's money) took place slowly over a five-year period I found it bearable—and possible to keep the dream alive. The wolf wouldn't easily blow down the straw house built on the sands of my cloud-cuckoo-land. One perfect omelet does not make a super chef nor does a business failure make you a bum. Read Harry Truman's autobiography.

Rationalization can be another explanation of why the entrepreneur must be radically obstinate. However, relying on "common-sense" got Britain into hot soup prior to World War II when her leaders sought to appease Adolph Hitler. Had it not been for Winston Churchill's obstinacy, the Brits might have had to develop a taste for sauerkraut and sausage.

Thomas Edison once said he tested his theories on the incandescent light bulb more than 3,000 times before he achieved success. Had he tried only 2,999, I might be composing this manuscript by computerized candlelight.

Just keep on truckin' and if you don't run out of gas, you, too, can learn to speed shift with either hand.

I've talked about how about how Don not only suggested a newspaper for me but he would finance the startup. I don't want to be flippant here, or leave anyone dismissing the scratch to start a business. Starting with scratch, as I said earlier, is difficult, but starting without it is impossible. And if you wait for your own miracle banker to come along and offer you a golden future, you may start to have doubts about my veracity. First thing is you can't sit around waiting for a timely miracle. They don't work that way. They sneak up on you when you aren't looking for them—kind of like graduating from puberty. What you have to do is keep an open mind and listen for the winds of the unnatural.

Besides, Don has retired and I'm thinking there aren't too many other bankers out here that realize how important, yes, even critical advertising in a weekly newspaper is to the continued health of their bulging vault.

Chapter 32

This whole exercise in prose has been about miracles and how you can't predict them but you should learn to recognize them when they peep out at you. However, even if you are inundated with miracles, (of course, that *would* be a fair-sized miracle) you still have to use the opportunity wisely. Through my experiences I now know that ignoring miracles is unproductive. Well, wasting them is, too. If not a sin, it's a terrible waste of unused blessings.

When Dr. Lawrence Peter, author of "The Peter Principle," said "Don't believe in miracles—depend on them," he was talking about an attitude change. Depend on miracles? Well, I admit I did not for the first several years of my working life, but later on when I had learned miracles *do* happen, I did and I still depend on them. It sounds goofy, but it is true if you look for them. Saying "Thank you, Lord," is the only way I know of to gain that unimaginable blessing; by expanding your mind and opening your heart to make room for the unusual. Take a flyer.

Back to the secular world, the first thing to do after you get that great idea is plan how you're going work the caper? You could always get a job and save your money but by the time you have enough, the government will have devalued your savings through inflation of the dollar...or some other dithering decision. Haste makes waste but dawdling usually means you come in second. Your Grand Opening might be your sell-by date.

There's always the chance to borrow from the mob, but if you do, remember: They take more interest in their interest than they do in your *very on time* payments. So if you are gonna do a newspaper, the mob is gonna want your barrel of newspaper ink as collateral. That may inhibit production somewhat unless you make a zillion dollars on your first issue, which would be somewhat happenstance and not bloody likely.

Begging your poor and middle class siblings to loan you money is not a good idea either. If you weren't friendly before, you'll be adversaries when you lose all their money. By that I mean your brothers and sisters will be reluctant to sue you. They'll rather shoot you.

You could blackmail someone. Most people have something to hide and if you judiciously allude to some inside information you've picked up, maybe you'll score. But that's risky. Of course, blackmail takes some expertise—and usually by the time you've got everyone and everything in place, you'll probably have used up more money than you'd have needed to launch your legitimate business. But maybe there's some excitement by doing it that way. If you really need thrill that badly, maybe you're not equipped to run a valid enterprise anyway.

If you are desperate, there's always your congressman. Usually you don't have look past their early morning shower before you find their hidden "tattoos." But that's not really fair, picking on your congressman. You can't take pride in taking advantage of your congressman's many foibles. True achievement is measured by the effort expended and most congressmen are such easy targets for dilly dolling or whatever, you'll feel unrequited by your success.

True tranquility and satisfaction only count when you've still got integrity after the dust settles.

And finally, to raise money for your venture, don't depend on prayer. Praying for money is wrong because God doesn't fund businesses. God does provide enablement for an honorable pursuit. And that's better than money or good luck. Think about it.

Be aware and ready, though; don't overlook any opportunity…well, maybe ignore those letters from the scoundrel who wants access to your bank account entirely. That's too good to be true. I mean, how does he know you won't abscond with that $30 million the day after he deposits it in your account? Never deal with an admitted public servant.

Chapter 33

Here is some advice you won't get from your friendly college professor of business.

Always keep your goal in mind (if you don't have a goal, make one up). No one will loan you money if you don't have a goal, f'r cryin' out loud. And you don't have to be truthful when your business plan is being perused by a bank loan officer—who may (or may not realize your unique astuteness, but what the hell, it's only business...). He's holding your world in his careless-portfolio-fumbling greedy fingers that were educated to make money for his bank and if you can help, well, maybe he'll give you a loan. If you have to admit later you lied, that will come at the bankruptcy hearing when your honor doesn't matter anymore.

I have heard, although I can't reveal my source, that banking rules written by the FDIC are second only in rigidity to that of a U.S. Army Special Ops squad heading to bad guy country. In other words, don't screw around. Your banker is obligated by the U.S. Government to tighten the noose on naughty clients just as surely as a GI must pull the trigger on a crazed terrorist. It's a duty, you know, to survive.

Therefore, always treat your loan officer with just as much respect and awe as you would a burley sergeant in your kitchen opening a can of beans with his teeth while holding a grenade launcher.

There are so many ways being a small newspaper adventurer can get his or her jollies. Oh, the perks! If you pick the right political position, you'll probably meet the mayor. The city council will ask you for free ink. If you're in the wrong camp, they won't bother you as much—but they won't give you any little pre-tips on news, either. (Check the voter registration records in your intended distribution area before you declare your true colors. And don't worry if you have to fib a bit. Truth gets sort of squishy when dealing with politics.)

You'll often be sent free tickets for concerts and circuses, most of which if you were teaching eighth grade physics you'd never even be invited to, let alone get a free pass.

One of the biggest perks will often fool you and you'll believe it's a miracle. That is when you suddenly attain the stature of a sagacious wit about town. Once you start calling yourself "editor," people will often believe you know how to spell sagacious. You'll be called for advice on weighty matters and be told really juicy items you won't be able to publish.

I've never reckoned too long on why people come to believe newspaper people are better informed, more objective and/or brainy. But then, after reading a blog or two on the net, I can understand. People who write are different from people who read. Many, many writers are opinionated, egotistic, judgmental and if careful in their prosey snideness, will never have to explain why they were following the local district attorney around and found to their aghastment that he can drink more than the reporter.

It's a wonderful position, that of editor or publisher. People just naturally think you know more than they do. I don't know why unless they still believe if you read it in the "paper," it must be true. Truth be known, you probably don't know as much but you get those anonymous tips and it makes you look like an oracle of some esteem. It's natural. If you suspect your neighbor is knocking off banks in his spare time, who else other than the local newspaper are you gonna call anonymously? You call the cops and next thing you know, they'll be asking for your name and identification which they swear will never be released. Unless a hacker gets into the police files, don't you know.

Good advice is, if you become an editor and people come to you believing you are well-informed, don't deny it. Of course, even if in all humility you deny you know who is being investigated by a really powerful Washington bureau, you are ahead of them on where the investigatee is hiding, they won't believe you anyway. You, dear sir or madam editor, *know*! They think you just won't tell until you've published it, dang your secretive hide.

Daily newspapers have their problems these days. Weeklies...? Well, you won't find many in financial trouble if they are judicious in their dealings with the public. Dealings with the government, however, can get a small weekly in big trouble. Government does not think, act, eat, sleep, wool gather or even spit like a civilian. Government exists only in a vacuum of regulation.

There are some small newspapers that make money off the government, legal notices and such, but they are mostly owned and run by those who would rather make money than enjoy putting out the weekly news just for the satisfaction of informing, entertaining and impugning the fallible county parks board for watering the parks too much or too little. (Why anyone would volunteer their leisure time to sit on any civic board is they are either very lonely or actually believe they might have a say in their city/county government. Volunteer once and you'll understand what I've just declared. You are there—appointed or elected—because *someone* has to take the flak for what the public servants screw up.)

No matter what kind of small business you pursue, always consider that the government is just as interested in your success or failure as your heirs. Government makes a living out of living off your efforts and even if you fail, government will still get a piece of you. Insolvency is not recognized by government, judicial or ruling politician. It cannot exist in the minds and hearts of those who need our money to screw up in the first place.

Give it a shot anyway. If you have a good tax attorney and accountant, you might beat the "public servants" at their own game: Take deductions as though you were picking daisies among the poison ivy. And watch out for perks, such as your congressman or woman actually admitting you exist and are worthy of acknowledgment. In the newspaper business, I learned that politicians will take note of you when they're bored or out of junket funding and will sometimes invite you to visit their anointed offices where they'll ask you discerning questions which, if you bother to answer, they'll be joking about over cocktails soon after you've been wished a good trip home.

In a newspaper, even though you want to keep to your principles, you'll unintentionally become involved in politics. Comes with the ink; you have it, they want it. It took a few years after launching the newspapers for me to come to the conclusion that politicians abuse their power indiscriminately while at the same time try to be fair to all. Soon the Editions policy became that you should never give a politician an even break because you'll never break even.

Even more important, before you decide to do government contract work, test yourself. Do you have the personality and inclination to answer such questions as: Who owns your newspaper? Have you ever been arrested for letting your passport expire?

What was your father's chosen deodorant? Did he chew tobacco?

Okay, those samples of tribulation are a little bit selective, but government can cause you mental stress that, if you only sell classified ads, you may feel like blowing up the local city hall. It isn't worth it. Someone will suggest a new tax to rebuild it. Government is difficult, not only to *be au fait with*, but to businessize with. When's the last time your congress personage delivered anything with which you could make money in a small newspaper—or any small business? Huh?

Ironically, when I first contemplated becoming a news person, I had a purpose. I thought it would be of public benefit to keep some space open for local and state politicians to explain to our readers why or why not they did or didn't do this or that or vote thisaway or thataway.

Took two years to realize that politicians were more interested in finagling the voters into voting aye just so's they could get elected to continue a career in finagling. And, too, when they did deign to send a bit of communication, they mostly wrote about other straying pols, probably to make themselves look or feel better.

Additionally, trying to deal with, understand or profit from doing business with the government was an awfully time consuming and disheartening exercise in frantic frustration. We once got a request from the local army post for a subscription to our newspaper. We were flattered that the U.S. Army had noticed we existed. When the request came in the mail, we were perplexed, bamboozled and looking for a good therapist. Here's how it happened:

> *Purchase order disorder*
> *(Please complete and return the enclosed form:)*
> *Form 21120266459lw.*
> *BPOENRABEDAMNED—*
> *23skiddoo....~~~~~*
>
> *Now I know we've all heard the stories of horrendous waste and mismanagement, even fraud, in the Department of Defense. Remember the $700 hammer to build the $600 toilet?*
>
> *Don't believe it. It's all a myth. When I was fighting the war, I learned it's sinful for our government guardians to not "overspend" tax dollars. And it's danged hard not to cheat, although I admit I've yet to meet that GI who really did ship a jeep home in pieces through the U.S. Mail (old GI joke.)*

However, I knew a couple ambidextrous nose-pickers who tried, but neither could determine how to get the drive shaft into a footlocker (1 ea. GI portable closet; box for mailing purloined government property to permanent home address; convenient storage locker for dirty laundry). But it isn't the GIs down the line who cost taxpayers; it's the professionals who have mastered the game of foraging on United States Official Property. It's done by regulation, or more specifically writing rules that no civilian has the patience to read.

Just recently, I had an experience demonstrating the judicious diligence that goes into government purchasing. We received a notice that Fort Carson would like to buy a subscription to the Edition. Not a large purchase—only three fins a year. But I was willing to take a shot at federal bucks. There is absolutely no way we could defraud the U.S. Army regarding the expenditure of that fifteen bucks. It makes me proud to be an American.

The request came by way of seven (7-ea) pages of forms. First was the "SF 30(Rev. 10-83 prescribed by GSA FAR(48CFR)53.243 Previous Edition Unusable" which is titled the "Amendment of Solicitation/Modification of

Contract." Accompanying this initial two-page form is DD Form 1155, Jul 87, Order for Supplies or Services Form approved DMB No. 0704-0817 Expires Jul 31 1989" which has (on the first page) forty-two spaces to be filled in with information even my doctor doesn't have.

Then there are two pages of "Clauses Incorporated by Reference (FAR 52-252-002) (Jun 88)" which seem to require a list of what the "contract" incorporates, items like equal opportunity gratuities, convict labor, etc. The next to the last page is headed: "Contract Clause and Solicitation Provision Numbering," which begins with: "This document is computer generated..." I didn't read the rest.

The last page, which I finally got to over Sunday morning coffee, is, I think, some information required about invoicing. I dunno.

Seven pages to be read, blanks to be filled, signature blocks to be scribbled, and mailed in a large wooden truck box to the U.S. Army. This for the price of a tetanus shot.

The problem here is I don't know for sure what all I'm telling the army. With all those blank blanks, I could end up in the National Guard and I'm not even One-A anymore.

Government forms have always chilled me, ever since I had to fill out a "preference" form for an Air Force overseas assignment fifty years ago, about the same time Khrushchev had to buy new shoes to replace those he'd worn out on the UN table when he wanted to bury the American Ambassador along with the rest of us.

The military form included several choices and slots, one being something about Merrill's Marauders in Burma, B Team, and "Walk a Mile on the Beautiful 38th Parallel." Hah! I knew what those assignments entailed. When I got to the one that offered free skiing, I checked the box...and ended up in Airman's Paradise, Thule, Greenland, right next to the ice cap that certainly wasn't melting when I was there. (There was no skiing in Thule, except when the wind blew—often—hard—unforgiving—and the end of the "slope" as any intrepid skier should be aware, which, if the wind is just right, might lead you miles out on the sea ice heading for New Jersey.

I almost didn't sign my discharge papers. Once bitten, and all that. My hand was trembling so much, the wave-goodbye-officer couldn't read my signature and I was almost extended for two months to ascertain whether I was psychologically fit for life in Jockey white underwear.

Enjoying my life of freedom to choose, I sent Fort Carson a gratis subscription. I should live so long.

-30-

Chapter 34

Big lesson here. Along with perquisites, there are vexations, one being a dearth of vacations. Working sixty to seventy hours a week might, and I emphasize MIGHT, bring success. However, if you are always working, you probably won't appreciate your slow, tortuous climb toward success and will continue working those long hours until you have a nervous breakdown. Or you get into the unpaid overtime weekend habit and when success does come along, you're too habituated to skipping meals and/or weekends off to notice you're not sleeping on your feet anymore.

Our first three or four years were marked with a hurried weekend or two in Denver in a "moderately priced" hotel. We ate at Doug's Diner and Cheap Jewelry Emporium. It was probably eight or nine years before Carolyn and I felt we could take a vacation: Three days in Las Vegas. And what did I do? Mostly wonder how the newspaper would survive me being gone a whole Monday. It wasn't a vacation. It was adding to my worry time! I spent two whole days stuffing slot machines with the quarters I'd taken out of the newsstands.

We never revisited Vegas. I lost $10 in a slot and that meant it was a good thing we'd purchased round trip air fares. It also meant Carolyn continued to darn my socks and I edged the lawn with my hunting knife.

Your business is more likely to fail when you, through a lack of "doodle time," a time of no-think, think wrong or not thinking at all. Working twenty-four-seven can put you in a rut so deep, even your accountant won't be able to locate your assets under that pile of worry, sweat, hooha and missteps caused by unrelieved ruttiness.

Take the time off! Trade your worries for an open Interstate Highway going 75 mph while dodging diesels; leave your domineering world behind. For instance, class reunions are fun and usually cheap unless you've mortgaged the house to impress your former friends who predicted you would only succeed if you married well. Go! Brag about your success. Who's gonna know? Or care?

My fortieth class reunion was, I think, most successful because I had just completed a creative writing course at the local community college. Two weeks' intensively creating fiction and anyone can coerce themselves into believing fantasies are not just for Walt Disney. You, too, can be a success in those little bios you send to the reunion organizers; it just takes the right thought patterns and sometimes, it can open new horizons. Remember how Thomas Edison dreamed up the light bulb? And don't worry about details like he made bulbs before light switches were invented. Tom invented those, too. He was probably bragging at his high school reunion when the idea (flash) came to him.

Or, on t'other hand, some time away gives you more time for uninterrupted worrying. That works, too, because the increased fretting will see you home with a newness of purpose: Desperation is a stupendous motivator but it is not advised here. I determined to attend my reunion.

Sixth graders! Plan your 40-year class reunion now

I went to my high school reunion recently and I haven't had so much fun since I walked into the girls' locker room by mistake.

So maybe this is the proper time to advise students on their pursuit of education. The first advice is to all sixth-graders. Never make fun of the ugliest or the dumbest kid in your class because that's the one who will end up as the prettiest or the richest...or an IRS auditor.

And don't be a drop-out because then you might be too embarrassed to attend your class reunions where you can impress your old classmates with your maturity and good sense...and gloat over having picked the prettiest or handsomest spouse there.

And lastly, memorize all your classmates' names because it is embarrassing to not recognize your best friend of forty years ago just because she or he lost their hair, teeth or ability to feed themselves.

When I got to the "ice breaker" party, I didn't even recognize my own senior picture which had been thoughtfully pasted to a card bearing my name so it could be pinned to my jacket which I had purchased from a very exclusive tailor for this occasion so that I could impress people whom I haven't seen for forty years and who couldn't care less that I have this very expensive jacket which was tailor-made for me because they were too busy hoping I would notice their very expensive jacket made by an exclusive tailor who…

It wasn't all fun, though. There was the moment when I introduced myself to an old girl-friend. Her confused expression was quickly replaced by a broad grin. Then she turned to her husband. "Oh, look, dear…ha ha. Look who's here. Ha ha ha. This is my…ha ha.. Can you believe it? I thought I loved…ha ha (choke) … ha ha. I just can't believe…ha ha…Oh, I'm so sorry….hoohahaha… I just can't see…ha ha… seem to stop…ha ha."

It would have been less mortifying if I had glanced down and noticed my fly was open so I could have had an honorable excuse to go to the men's room. Another curious thing was that all my old classmates remembered that I was the fastest runner in the sixth grade. No one seemed to recall that I was still around in high school. I had disappeared from their conscious minds for forty-six years!

Even when I reminded them that I was president of the debating team (a lie), or that I set

*the state record for spikes (we didn't have a vol-
leyball team), or that I was the lead dancer in
the senior class production of "An American in
Paris" (which we didn't perform), no one seemed
to notice. "You remember ol' Hank could outrun
the whole football team?" "Oh, yeah, ha ha, he
was sure a swift fella, all right."*

*A really successful class reunion is when you
have some classmates who achieve a measure of
fame or notoriety or who have become someone or
something unusual. One old friend brought his
"first" wife and seemed happy with her company.
We had an ex-NFL defensive back that probably makes more money from his players' pension
than the rest of us will earn in the next forty
years.*

*There was the Vietnam combat veteran who
didn't have even one flashback. We had one from
an earlier reunion who didn't show up because
he was being sought by a very large government
agency. He is now in a highly protected environment that doesn't allow pizza delivery.*

*And the quiet folks were still quiet, not brag-
ging at all about their success even though they
came in automobiles that were larger than my
newspaper delivery truck.*

The class became more dignified as the years rolled by. The beer keg was over half full when the party broke up. Forty years ago, there would have several guys still sucking at the nozzle, trying to drag out one last drop for the road. No one took a swing at the disc jockey who played the "nostalgic" music loud enough for any present-day rocker—and who had obviously never heard of Johnnie Ray or Vaughn Monroe or the Mills Brothers or Teresa Brewer. His loss.

Reunions are uplifting. No matter how tough the last forty years may have been, it can be one big ego booster. Remember this, young students: No lie is too big to be told after 40 years of absence from one another. Of course, you have to be selective in describing all your college degrees and all the honors you've received. Be sure to name schools in Middle Eastern countries that have been "couped" a few times where all the universities have been burned down along with your scholastic records.

Use lots of heavily intellectual words to describe your accomplishments.

Try this one. "Well, yes, I studied the ancient Zimwall Boomsha in Farthanlower Campoodle. We, er, uh, found evidence of the curly-nosed Wang Chi species which led to several contiguous fellowships at Notre Dame where we were able to protract evidentializing the tendential effects of contrived cross-breeding with the pork-tailed Khadafi Whalloper."

Let 'em try to check that out.

-30-

Chapter 35

That class reunion may have been a wake-up call to do something about my impecuniousness. We can't tell whether old classmates are successful or good actors. Just a bit risky; someone once said a fool can't be an actor but an actor can play the fool. I may be an exception.

I struggled on for many months trying every method I could steal from successful businesses to make the Edition pay enough to at least take Carolyn out of the rat race for a long weekend, even if it was only the 1920s cabin court across the street from the not too often but enough landings/takeoffs to keep you awake airport landing (one a night) in Gunderson, Kansas.

I also about that time began to get serious about my prayers. Mostly I'd always prayed for a winning lottery ticket or at least something of secular value that couldn't be traced by the law. But without knowing it was happening, I began to pray for guidance and wisdom. I had gone through life thus far with a wispy belief that, despite a pretty good IQ noted in high school, I probably was a bit lazy and not inclined toward enlightenment; rationalization is much easier.

Miracles were still on my menu, however. What happened was, one day my phone rang and the caller was one of the big and successful home developers. I knew who he was but I don't think we'd ever shared a conversation. Dave asked how was business and I lied and said fine. Obviously he knew better. Then he surprised me by inviting me to drop by his office when I had some free time. Free time? That was about all I had free in those days.

Trying to remain suave and sound proficiently professional, I found an open date in my appointment calendar, which at that time the margins in the newspapers could take care of. I went anxiously to his office two days later and Dave dropped one on me. He said he liked our newspaper and would like to buy yearly subscriptions to go to all the new homes on his thirteen hundred acres or so development of more-than-median-income families.

I sat very still in my chair, trying to be business man like and not jump over his desk and kiss him. What in the world had prompted his call? What exquisite timing it had to be to renew the hope I had misplaced for my and mine's future.

The incident, the re-inking of my soul, so to speak, didn't make much sense but I wasn't even thinking of the whys. I took the check and soared to the bank where I sniffed snidely as I danced across the lobby and by the loan officer's hidey hole and up to the cashier's counter. *I was solvent again!* At least temporarily.

It was a couple years before I candidly began to question my past rendezvous with good, timely and unearned good luck. But there it was, upon reflection, another in a line of miracles. Although I had thanked Dave for his grubstake, it was then I *really* began to thank God for his blessings to me.

It must have been a well experienced Christian who expressed this truth: "Your enjoyment of something doubles if you realize how lucky you are to have it." I was beginning to learn precisely what that sage had meant.

And then vacations start coming, right about the time we'd given in to forever being slaves to our business. Actually, Carolyn indicated she was taking one and I could come along or not. But she was taking the credit card with her. 'Course, she was also taking the car which meant it would be sort of foolish for me to stay home since that's where I'd be—staying home from work while she was having a good time at the seashore or something. On first thought, I decided it was a great idea.

From that day forward we took as much time off as conscience would allow. (Conscience, by the way, can get in the way of enjoying yourself. It should not be ignored. However, reasoning with it sometimes works.) Whatever you might have accomplished in that time, you still suspect time spent away from poorly paid serfmanship can be worth what you missed not running the ship of golden dreams.

Habits are hard to break and when you get too habituated to a work ethic, that's when you start growing old. So keep a lookout for that when you wake up and believe you should go to work and it's a holiday weekend. Growing old can easily become a habit and it's hard to break. More later on how to stay young—or at least how to convince yourself you earned all those wrinkles.

I believed Carolyn when she said she'd take the car, my beloved 1994 Buick Regal Custom with the sage green paint and light-up ashtray. I decided to go along, telling myself that I could use the time to explore that wonderful place where all the money goes to disappear into budgets that must be runneth over annually or our country will die!

The Land of the Lost

We are out of town on a trip Carolyn and I have long anticipated. We're visiting an enigmatic and some say, unusual part of our world. For a long time I've read about the "People to People" program where Americans are interacting with people of other climes via habitual handouts in an effort to achieve an understanding *of the way other people think, live and function. There seems to be no better way to build understanding than by getting folks together to look one another in the eye, communicate, exchange ideas and maybe explain why we are always ticked off at each other's government.*

Understanding is difficult if we hold ourselves aloof from people we consider a little looney or always wanting a piece of the U.S.'s action. It is my mission in life to discover why this is. The globe is shrinking and the only way we're going to survive is to learn how those "others" perceive folks like us Americans. It is also a good way to build cooperation in the pursuit of peace and goodwill, a so far daunting task.

So I bought a guidebook and a cross-language dictionary. I looked up the customs and history of the targeted area and tried to acclimate myself to the protocols necessary to avoid offending the natives.

Soon after arrival, I realized we were indeed on unfamiliar, even alien turf. The natives seemed frantic on a sort of frenzied, chaotic path, hurrying hither and yon while expressing harried facial expressions. They seemed shortsighted, even distracted. Everyone seemed to be scurrying to a destination that neither Carolyn or I could discern.

There seemed to be quite a few who had no place to go, staring off into space and twiddling with some sort of scepter. When I tried to engage some in conversation, my dictionary was of no help. They spoke a language that was vaguely familiar yet never seemed to talk directly to me. I asked one regal appearing gentleman if he could suggest where we might find accommodations. He replied that accommodations were a high priority in this land and, although he was sure we'd be taken care of, it was a matter of which direction we wished to take. "I'm sure we have just what you need but there are so many choices, you needn't worry. In fact, I think I have the answer." Then he turned and walked away without another word and before I could grab our luggage, he disappeared into large crowd circling aimlessly while talking to themselves.

There was no wind when we arrived but the inhabitants looked to walking with an inclination either to the left or the right. We saw very few on a healthy perpendicular bearing.

We were left wandering by ourselves, hoping to find some landmark that would give us a lead to an overnight dwelling place, a place that could provide comfort and security for outsiders like ourselves. Finally we spied a great spire that seemed to beckon lost souls in need of sustenance and validation. Vaguely, it reminded us of compassion, even reliance that once there must have been a preponderance of prescience prepense in this strange land.

We worked our way toward this reassuring symbol of haven but when we got closer, we could see its base was full of cracks and its foundation seemed to be wavering in mournful anticipation *of crumbling into a heaped mass of the misplaced dreams of a brave new but evaporating landscape of fog and deeper gathering of dark clouds.*

We finally found a place to lay our heads, a majestic relic of a more glorious past. We were escorted to an elegant suite with a large window overlooking the center of this busy metropolis and there, in the middle of this orgy of bumble and bustle, we saw it again. The Washington Monument, an aging symbol of a retreating but glorious experiment. Our sleep was haunted by a vision of decaying expectations.

-30-

We started out with small helpings of vacations or time away, right up to that Washington, DC. visit. At first, we felt we could barely afford the perks of travel, like eating. As for gas, we were in that time when nobody but an oil mogul could afford to drive outside the city limits. It was a time of darned socks and patched jeans.

To add to my unease about leaving the house before checking with my insurance agent, I began to injure myself. It was more than paper cuts. I'd bang my head or carelessly speed up my tooth brushing and poke the danged thing into a sensitive cavity. For awhile there I thought I was getting messages from that parallel world people talk about. I couldn't seem to go away without wounding myself first.

We planned a skiing trip and as we were leaving the house for the slope, I stepped on the frozen welcome mat wrongly and sprained my ankle. Don't ask. I knew the family would be really disappointed if we didn't go through with the trip, so I rented some crutches and we wended our way toward those ugly black clouds over the mountains.

It worked out rather well. When I checked in at the ski hotel on crutches, everyone in the lobby was sympathetic, figuring my injury was ski-caused. I didn't tell 'em better. So while the boys were skiing, Carolyn and I stayed in the lodge. Remarkable how a crutch or cast will draw admiring glances; sorta like a badge of courage. And, too, seemingly with a ski slope nearby, nobody thinks of you as a klutz. A clumsy amateur, maybe?

Through the years we timidly mastered the art of not leaving home without "it."("It" took a few trips before we got the hang of packing suitcases and leaving behind the heartbeat thrum-thrum of printing presses.) Although I felt just a bit uneasy about leaving the newspapers without my presence on the scene, those trips gave me more and more high and low jinks to write about in my weekly column. And, if I say so myself, the columns improved and readership went up. Many readers began to comment on the material I used in my humorous outlook on pseudo-serious daily life and my curious take on politics at the risk of my sanity.

Even when we got as far as East Africa on our jaunts, I never got over my surprise that, figuratively speaking, we had come so far. And yes, I considered the distance from my childhood expectations to actually being a world traveler. And I said, "Thank You."

Chapter 36

Amiracle in 1992 preserved my pride and entrepreneurship. A millionaire joined my Rotary Club. Most folks seem to consider Rotary to be a rich man's club, but it has changed over the years until it is now a haven for everyone from the hoi polloi to those who are called "filthy rich" by the intellectuals.

Stoney was a man who didn't see anything wrong with hanging out with folks who didn't talk stock marketese all the time. He was just as down to earth as any fella who could buy the building where Rotary was meeting.

For a long time I had no idea he was wealthy but one day I was bemoaning to a friend my waning possibilities for accumulating some of that filthy lucre Bill Gates and Sam Walton send to starving Africans. My friend suggested I talk with Stoney. I was put off by the notion; rich guys know more ways to say no than a bank loan officer with a toothache.

The newspapers were barely making their own way financially. Problem was, if we had two bad ad sales weeks, we'd be out of business. One way to perk up the accountants and bankers was to show a reasonable profit for the next quarter. How do I do that?

One tried-and-true way to increase readership for our advertisers' benefit was to increase our publication numbers. The more readers, the more advertisers would love our newspaper. We'd been limping along with a press run down to about 1,500 papers delivered to neighborhood homes. The "Catch 22" larger printing totals we needed were way more expensive and I knew we needed numbers in the 5,000 to 7,500 range.

So I girded myself in pica poles, rubbed printer's ink on my forehead and made sure to sit next to Stoney at the next week's Rotary meeting. After the meeting, I grabbed Stoney by the arm and said something like, "Mr. Kahn, would it be possible you might be interested in a capitalistic venture that is worth its weight in golden prose?"

Fortunately, Stoney was the adventurous sort, although he may have taken it as an opportunity to learn whether I was an entrepreneur or a big mouth jerk. Millionaires just instinctively know how to enjoy themselves. We had our chat. Stoney thought it over for a week or so and then called.

Even though he didn't know me, he'd seen the newspaper. He said, "Okay, I'll back you this much. But I give you a fifty-fifty chance you'll ever pay me back." His offer was below my hopes but not my dignity. Furthermore, Stoney's sparse offer coupled with my thoroughly forlorn mood at the time just might be enough to prolong the flow of news for another six months.

Yes, I was insulted but I took the check. It was an honorable gamble since for most of my life I hadn't been tilted toward accepting challenges unless they didn't involve sweating or cogitation to deeper levels of commitment than that with which I was comfortable. Stoney had challenged me and this time I took the challenge. I determined to work yet harder and a lot smarter than my comfort level. My adopted lifestyle of floating blithely through life had been fun, but aging means more than your organs slowing down; in the past several months all my airy cloud Nines had begun to shrink, too.

After almost a decade, Stoney's investment paid off for him as well as for me. Was Stoney yet another miracle? Of course he was and his bit of financial gaming ultimately was responsible for some miraculous seven figure annual ad sales. It would also lead to fantasies about the possible retirement of a very fortunate publisher/editor. Me. Just a few years more and it might happen.

Chapter 37

At sixty-five I began to suspect my personal cloud was drooping a bit. And I suspected my miracles might be numbered. It wasn't the way I felt or functioned. It was looking into the mirror while shaving and noticing that the bags could be recycled at Wal Mart. I was beginning to look hoary on the outside and if that was any measure of what my insides looked like, maybe I should take another look at that Sears hammock I'd always wanted. I was never one to check my reflection closely, but the mirror insisted. Oh, there were other things to consider. My plainness wasn't that noticeable as I slowly wrinkled up. It didn't help when I received a notice from the government that I was of an age they would like to send back some of the money I'd "invested" in Social Security.

Yet, retirement didn't appeal one way or another. I still thought I was having fun. I kept convincing myself that Andy at forty-three just *wasn't ready* to take over the whole business. Many of us confuse sweat equity with the growth of wisdom which then leads to a sense of our self importance and we end up feeding our ego trans fats.

So I hung around in the belief that since *I* was the founder, I was the only person who knew all the secrets of Walter Publishing and why it had become so profitable. It took that long to absorb that it was all those other people in and out of the place that were making things hum along. With that tiny bit of gristle to chew, I knew everyone knew more than me…and sooner. I am a slow learner.

It took five more years before veracity demolished my mental blockade. One day Andy answered the phone and talked for a couple minutes to I don't remember who. He turned to me and said, "Dad, do you want to talk to this guy?" I took the phone and in less than a minute I realized I had no idea what he was talking about. I said I'd get back to him and then turned to and humbly admitted to

Andy that he knew more about what the guy was proposing than I.

Andy explained to me exactly what the caller was proposing and then turned back to his own work. I stared at him for a few minutes and there it was: My son knew more about publishing than I did. But he was not going to assert any leadership as long as the old man was across the office decomposing. He was unconsciously propping me up in the never ending struggle against dotagehood! My pride was hurt, my muse was requiring more and more prescriptions and my memory was fogging up even on the clearest days.

The time had come, the old walrus said, to make himself scarce. Since I had no plans for entertaining myself with five extra Saturdays, I continued to procrastinate. I kept making excuses to myself that only I knew how to keep track of the back issues in the morgue.

Things became clear when I had to have a heart bypass. No big deal, actually; my heart was good but its supply lines were becoming like rush hour traffic, very slow. Three days took care of the affliction, but that same three days introduced me to my mortality. What if I died before we published our next issue? Andy would have to make all the decisions and deliveries to the carriers of news that was fit to print. Holy Cow! Yes, he could!

The age of seventy is not a bad time as long as you don't carelessly flush your meds. But seventy is also a time a fella should enjoy sitting on his laurels while contemplating all the world's problems he had solved. I began to count. When I got to one, I realized the world was much messier than it was when I started telling all our readers that politicians were superfluous. The politicians had long since learned the tricks of larceny, even better than the Mob.

I kept telling myself it would be good, that I'm lucky to be an American and was able to retire before I died or the IRS put a lien on my body parts.

And then... It happened again; another episode completely foreign to my mind. A little background here is relevant. Budgeting, saving, looking for the best bargain... those activities had never appealed to me because it was easier not to plan past Tuesday, as I've noted before. Frugality and preparation was for people who already had money. But then a gentleman had induced me to trust him as my stockbroker. It was rather out of character for me, but I agreed—reluctantly—to part with some money. Buying things I couldn't see, smell or taste! Even though the stock market had been kind to me, and even though like many others I expected it to just keep growing, somehow a doubt began to grow.

I invested a few bucks and then a few more. Surprising my inner devil doubters, I did well in the market. There was that beginner's luck again. (?) Nothing miraculous but certainly, for me, a deeper understanding of how things work. As a banker once told me, he had the best job in the world because he made money while he slept. Now, I thought, looking at money made sans no honest effort, I got it.

Chapter 38

After five years in withdrawal, I have to admit had I known the joy of immeasurable loafing, I would have retired when I was sixteen. I mean, at this stage of life, even if your health isn't great, you know you don't have to get out on those winter mornings to go to work when your arthritic knees hurt. It's easier to find the positive if you cope dexterously.

It was then I got my first cell phone. The family insisted. Although I was of sound mind and body, my behavior and acceptance in this high tech world had been unsettling to them. See, I gave up early on trying to understand how computers (so I'm told) can fly airplanes, mix paint and get people dates. I think the family wasn't being kind so much as wanting to not waste gas tracking me down. "Please, dad, take it with you! And don't turn it off."

The trouble with kids is they don't want us old folks making decisions on our own because we might change our will. At seventy-five, I'd just about decided I could safely make my own decisions. (Help! I've fallen and I don't care if I get up. Nothing brings serenity more than knowing there's no one gonna help you, so you might's well take a nap.) At three score plus fifteen, if you haven't earned that right, you still deserve it by default.

I have complied with their wishes although I use a "traditional" phone, even if I have to drive a mile or two to find one. It's not so much fear of progress as it is trying to figure out how the hell to make a call on this young-at-heart piece of computerized closeness. The first time it rang in my pocket, it was on the buzzer. I almost tinkled in my pants.

No one needs to tell me how many old coots just like me play this digital world game with ease and comfort, getting their jollies by ordering their Viagra or Depends on-line. It's not that I envy them. It's just that at our age, instead of getting stressed and cursing our computer illiteracy, we should be enjoying the sunsets and an evening toddy while delightfully contemplating our trip to the next world—which I'm praying doesn't have fax machines or campaign promises.

What my family, and I'd bet many families, doesn't understand is that I've gotten no older since I was sixty. I'm on bonus miles. I've been rebooted, so to speak. If I want to stay in touch, I'll move in with the kids.

Young people don't fear getting old. That comes to them about two or three weeks before thirty-nine. They think it's just hang time until you croak, and that's sad. They're missing the point, which is, after sixty you should begin to realize, remember and appreciate all the miracles with which your life has been blessed.

The day I made my big announcement, no one said much, just "Okay, what will you do? Will you still write your column?" "When…?" am I going to retire? There was only one tear and it was in *my* eye. I knew they loved me. I knew they'd depended upon me for over twenty-five years to right the boat when the waves of despair and lousy ad sales flowed over us. I'm sure of it, no matter what they say now.

It was like, yeah, they needed me to clean the bathrooms and make sure coffee wasn't too weak. There was no pause in phone sales calling or employees signing out of the office. After that moment of silence, normal conversation began again and I was left to wander back to my desk thinking "I really don't know these people." But they were good at what they did.

As I've said, I hadn't really considered over-the-hill loafing, at least personally. Others could do it if they wanted, but I wasn't ready for elderly unemployment. I guess I never really believed the newspapers would make money. I'd end up in an urn stashed and forgotten in the newspaper's morgue. One day a friend came by and asked when I was going to get around to retiring. Told him I was about ready. He asked what I was going to do. I had no idea.

The next day he brought in a book on "How to Retire with Dignity." First chapter asked me the first question: What was I passionate about?

Hmmm. Uh. Nothing other than just keeping the newspaper solvent, but I was not "passionate" about it. Frightened, yes, but... I was passionate about my family, but they were doing okay even though they never had taken my cultured advice seriously. I never did get passionate about Carolyn's cats. That was a whole 'nother emotion that I couldn't talk about—except to the cat when Carolyn wasn't around.

I retired on April Fool's Day. I didn't mean it as a message. It just happened that the night before I'd gotten a call from a reader expressing great distress that I had not written a story about his daughter who won a three-legged race at her grammar school. I politely declined to publish it on the basis of not ridiculing his three-legged daughter. Some parents just have no clue, y'know.

So I went out the door for the last time. Well, not really but it was my avowed intention to not come back to the office until I could cope with and conquer those Golden Years and make myself believe I really deserved to lay in bed until nine a.m. and spend the next hour or so doing the daily crossword puzzle. Then maybe having another cuppa before I called someone to meet me for another cuppa at the restaurant where Don, the miracle banker, had unknowingly changed my life, my outlook, my belief in God and my willingness to search a great faith.

An astute retiree takes that old to-do list and crumples it jovially into a do-not-bother-me list. Sometimes I mowed the lawn—when I felt the urge or the cat got lost in the tall grass. I was retired. I **LOVED** IT! I now had five Saturdays to not go grocery shopping, to not grumble about Monday morning. Not try to paint the whole house on a weekend. I even went down and mowed the church lawn. (I'd never driven a rider mower before; and although I scraped the bricks and knocked the back fence cockeyed and tore one of the mower grass holders off, no one said anything. Probably because I was still cheaper than hiring a competent lawn service.

(If you haven't tried it, go borrow someone's riding mower. Even if it's not a Harley, you'll still feel like a silly kid again.)

I took Carolyn to Africa for three weeks, something she'd wanted to do since she was old enough to know she loved animals...any animal. It was wonderful. I was bored. But I loved to watch her as she watched the animals: Elephants, lions, hyenas, crocodiles...big ugly spiders on the tent wall. (Well, there was no love lost there, at least.) My problem was, if you see one elephant poop, you've seen a natural wonder of nature. Why look for more? Yes, life as a valid vagrant is wonderful.

Other things have happened. Since that young boy with the basketball walked by me that night of my grandson's school program, I've felt a confidence in myself that eluded me for most of my life. A confidence that everything I do is for the furtherance of God's holy plan. And for that reason, I'm no longer afraid to speak my mind at meetings. When I have to speak to my church congregation as their president, I don't worry that they might think me ill equipped or uncertain. I just don't fret.

I have a new life and I love it. I didn't hate my old life; I just tolerated it. I'm no longer a "spectator" Christian. And I no longer have doubts about my belief. In other words, I have been blessed even though in my own mind I know I haven't really earned it.

So many things have happened since I took notice of all the other earth dwellers. There are few (if any) I dislike today. Irritants are fewer and music is sweeter. Food tastes better and I hardly ever receive poor service. Waitresses are hard workers who deserve a good tip.

I've found others, too, have opinions. And they aren't all flawed.

Cats can be loving. Ice cream doesn't just taste good; it can be savored.

It's fun to be thankful when you realize all for which you have to be thankful. I never used to say an evening prayer but after reviewing my good fortune, I never miss saying a bedtime prayer. It is: God, thank you for running my cup over with blessings and joy even if there is absolutely no natural reason for it.

I've always loved my wife but these days of state-of-the-art hanging out are even more precious when I'm with her. It's almost like God so loved the world, He showed me a better way.

In all my meandering thoughts these days, one thing stands out. The drastic changes in my life and attitude since I awakened to the almost unbelievable possibilities God has shown me weren't a matter of maturation or gaining street smarts. Who else in the course of human events could have voiced so clearly and so out of this world the words, "Heaven's Better?"

Since I heard that, I realize that I can hardly wait.

* * *

Acknowledgments

I would like to acknowledge those with whose help this book finally came into print. Carolyn Walter without whom I would have given up were it not for her editing and proofreading and eternal support. Also, Reverend Dr. Erwin "Ob" Spruth and his wife, Joyce for taking their time to read and encourage my efforts. And who could ever forget the U.S. Congress who provided such great analogies for reality. Finally, the best ever muse and partner any of us could have, The Holy Spirit.

Hank Walter
Cover by Thomas McComb IV

Made in the USA
San Bernardino, CA
27 December 2012